SUCCESSION PLANTING
for
Year-round
Pleasure

Christopher Lloyd

Edited by
Erica Hunningher

Photographs by
Jonathan Buckley

SUCCESSION PLANTING
for Year-round Pleasure

Timber Press
Portland, Oregon

First published in 2005
Text copyright © Christopher Lloyd 2005
The moral right of the author has been asserted

Photographs copyright © Jonathan Buckley 2005,
except for one photograph by Fergus Garrett on pages
34–5 (centre) and two on page 184 (below right, top
and bottom)

Published in North America in 2005 by
Timber Press, Inc.
The Haseltine Building
133 S.W. Second Avenue, Suite 450
Portland, Oregon 97204-3527, U.S.A.
www.timberpress.com

ISBN 0-88192-713-9

A catalog record for this book is available from the
Library of Congress.

Conceived and edited by Erica Hunningher
Commissioning editor: Vivien Bowler
Typographic styling by studioGossett
Designer: Ken Wilson
Production controller: Kenneth McKay

Set in Scala
Printed and bound in Great Britain by Butler & Tanner
Colour separations by Butler & Tanner
Jacket printed by Butler & Tanner

BBC
BOOKS

Half title page
Papaver commutatum 'Ladybird' and Gladiolus
communis subsp. byzantinus.

Title page
At the turn of May and June a batch of mixed foxgloves,
Digitalis purpurea, is at its peak in the Long Border,
while Siberian wallflowers, Erysimum × marshallii (syn.
E. × allionii), have already had a long season and are
preparing to pack it in. Allium cristophii, at bottom left,
is a great stalwart, flowering in June but retaining
its shape to the end of the season.

Contents page
A single ox-eye or moon daisy, Leucanthemum vulgare,
usually seen in a crowd.

CONTENTS

The art and craft of
SUCCESSIONS

One of our principal aims is to get year-round pleasure from our gardens by keeping the show going over as long a period as possible.

◀ *The early-summer out-burst of brilliant magenta* Gladiolus communis subsp. byzantinus *stops you in your tracks. There are some quite weakly coloured strains sold under this name – make sure you get the right one. The corms multiply rapidly to form colonies. Hardiness may be doubtful in cold areas. The gladiolus is growing here among dwarf bamboo,* Pleioblastus viridistriatus (syn. P. auricomus), *with leaves striped yellow and green; the colour is brightest if we have cut the canes to the ground in April.*

A continuous thread of successions, one highlight being immediately taken over by the next, is what we are after. My object in this book is to suggest how to plant so as to achieve this. For brevity, we often refer to it as succession planting. I am using my experiences at Great Dixter, in East Sussex, England, as a case study. Whatever your own circumstances may be – warmer, colder, less spacious, more spacious, never mind what – the principles of this sort of gardening remain the same.

At no point, at least from spring (early April for us) to autumn (end of October), but not forgetting the winter, shall there be a lapse, a hole in our armoury. No single group of plants can possibly achieve this, so we make use of every kind of plant that is available to us. This is the concept of the mixed border, which is not a new idea. Early in the twentieth century Gertrude Jekyll was using any plants, including small trees and shrubs, that would best sustain her colour vision. My own first book was entitled *The Mixed Border* and that was published some half century ago.

A mixed border offers the greatest scope, because in it you can include trees, shrubs, climbers, perennials (both hardy and tender), biennials, annuals, bulbs – the whole lot. There is no logical reason for restricting yourself. True, it is easier to imagine a single-content area. If, as has recently been fashionable, you plant an area entirely with ornamental grasses and other grass-like plants, the

concept is simple enough to grasp. But then, while acknowledging that grasses provide good contrasts to other types of plants, you come to realize that on their own they are too samey. They themselves are crying out for contrast. You come to long for some plants that are bolder, more solid.

We all want to grow roses, but seeing them herded together emphasizes their faults, like the blobby distribution of their flowers or their stiffness of habit, quite apart from the problems from pests and diseases that inevitably arise when one kind of living organism (it's the same with humans; one child at school gets mumps and they all get mumps) is herded into dense colonies. From this we mature and come to realize that access to all sorts of plants is the most rewarding. It requires more ingenuity but is a bottomless well of fascinating interest.

Shrubs provide structure and solidity, but by themselves are too earthbound and lack dynamism. An all-shrub border quickly bores. Herbaceous borders, by contrast, lack structure, though they provide seasonal colour. The dormant season that perennials pass through can be exploited by using balancing perennials or other plants. Thus a perennial that gives of its best in the first half of the year but then aestivates can be followed by some that are at their best from midsummer to autumn. This arrangement also works

in reverse. One or the other will probably be Big Brother; the second string ensures continuity.

Bedding out gives us splashes of colour in spring and summer and into autumn. It has flexibility, being quick and easy to change, but it does lack substance. Bedding makes you wait. It takes time to come to maturity. If you know what you want, you may have to raise it yourself from scratch. However, in a mixed border there are other distractions from the waiting.

Among the entertainers are self-sowers, which provide an element of improvisation. They dance through our borders. But they need the strictest control. Perhaps ninety-nine out of a hundred of each kind will need to be thrown out. But that one per cent – it may have had a brilliant idea of where to put itself that you wouldn't have thought of – will provide a thread of continuity and of originality that deserves to be cherished. It may be a tall plant at the border's margin, where things are expected to be short. Think about that. It might look excellent just there and it might flourish on the minimal competition from neighbours that it will find in a marginal position.

Climbers in your mixed border, both annual and perennial, have many assets, though some potential snags, too, as we shall see. If trained over shrubs, they can cover up low points; up a tall support (like a clematis up a pole), they will be making use of otherwise unoccupied space above the main border contents.

CONSIDER THE SITE

I shall take you through the Long Border at Dixter as an example. It faces southwest, so it is sunny but open to prevailing winds, although there is the protection of oaks at a distance. It is one-sided and backed by a yew hedge – on average 2.25m/7ft high – the best, since its leaves are small and unobtrusive but make an excellent dark background for almost any colour. The hedge is cut on a batter, which is to say the bottom is broader than the top. This means that light reaches the whole hedge, even at the bottom, so it does not go bare there, nor develop an overhang, as vertical hedges do. The hedge top is rounded, not flat and this precludes weight from snow from pushing it out of shape. Since yew roots are surface-feeding and greedy, my father, at the time that the garden was made, around 1912, had sheets of galvanized iron (1m/3ft wide and bent double at the top so as not to leave a sharp edge) installed vertically between hedge and border. They have lasted effectively ever since.

Aucuba japonica *is one of those shrubs loosely known as laurel. There are males and females. We have one of each making a firm end-stop to the Long Border.*

◀ **In February** *the berries on* Aucuba japonica f. longifolia *ripen at the same time as hybrid helle-bores are in flower at its feet. This laurel is a female which fruits freely if it has a male partner nearby. After flowering the hellebores need to be concealed.*

◀ ▼ **At the turn of May–June,** *here is the male spotted laurel to the left of* Aucuba japonica f. longifolia. *The hellebores in the foreground are masked by cornflowers, bedded out in April, and by the foliage of a Japanese anemone,* A. tomentosa. *The magenta* Gladiolus communis subsp. byzan-tinus *peps up this area.*

▼ **Late July** *and the laurels are virtually unchanged, but* Anemone tomentosa *is in flower with* Phlox paniculata. Eucryphia glutinosa *is flowering at the back.*

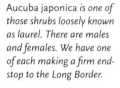

The border is fronted by a 1.5m/5ft-wide flagstone path of oblong Yorkstone slabs. (They at one time composed London paving until replaced by tar macadam.) There is then a strip of mown grass and beyond that a meadow.

The border is oblong and the main part of it is 63m/70yd long and 4.5m/15ft deep. There is a wide, Lutyens-designed oak seat at the top, the border being on a gradual rising slope. It is intersected two thirds of the way up by a cross-path leading to other parts of the garden.

The soil is clay-based – Wadhurst clay – so drainage is impor-tant and the soil is most effectively lightened by the addition, in large quantities, of coarse grit – the same grit as is recommended for the so-called sand element in John Innes composts. The soil has been enormously improved over the years by additions of organic manure and composts. Spent mushroom compost, which has taken a commercial crop of mushrooms, is strongly alkaline in reaction, so we have to take care to substitute decomposed bark, when operating close to calcifuge plants such as hydrangeas. Our natural pH is slightly more acid than neutral.

▶ **Early March**: *the border retains a variety of shapes and colours through the winter, even when there's no flower to be seen. There's the dark green conifer, Pinus mugo, in the foreground, next to spiky, orange-green leaves of New Zealand Libertia peregrinans, which are at their brightest in cold weather. Variegated Euonymus fortunei 'Silver Queen', spreading on to the path in the middle distance, is a year-round anchor plant. The evergreen aucubas beyond are the border's end-stops. At the border's edge Allium neapolitanum has had bright green, lanky grass-leaves since late autumn. The skeletons of last year's herbaceous plants, which look derelict at one moment but are transformed into objects of beauty by frost or snow, are soon to be swept away as we tackle a stretch of border at a time.*

▶ **Late March**: *the annual overhaul is complete, in time for opening the garden in April. Working from boards to avoid heavy plod marks, we have cut down last year's herbaceous debris, split and replanted perennials where advisable, and pruned deciduous shrubs where necessary. Self-sowers have been thinned and mushroom compost or composted bark has been tickled in with a long-handled, narrow, three-pronged fork. We have spread a dressing of Growmore at some 95g per square metre or 4oz to the square yard around the older shrubs that need it. Leaf buds are showing on deciduous shrubs and the ground is beginning to fill up with the fresh vegetation of perennials and bulbs. A clump of dark blue hyacinths (H. orientalis 'King of the Blues') can be seen at the front of the border. 'Delft Blue' hyacinths are at the top of the border among Japanese anemones. Too small to be visible in the photograph are cyclamen, snowdrops and self-sown primroses beneath the skirts of shrubs.*

▶ **Towards the end of April**: *tulips – we like single colours planted in natural-looking drifts – are at the height of their season, with our running theme of forget-me-nots, Myosotis, providing additional colour that lasts till the end of May. Watch the space towards the back of the border in this and the next pictures where the cardoon, Cynara cardunculus, is making low mounds of jagged, grey-green leaves that will be 3m/10ft, with candelabrums of mauve thistle-heads, in July and August. The foliage of poppies and alliums is evident already. The pale yellow young leaves of Spiraea japonica 'Gold Mound' look well next to the bronze evergreen foliage of Libertia peregrinans. Euonymus fortunei 'Silver Queen' still performs its role as a stylish anchor plant, but against the high wall dividing the upper and lower terraces, Magnolia × soulangeana 'Lennei' has started a great display which lasts for several weeks.*

◀◀ / ▶ **The last week of May**: *the anchor plants of* aucubas, Euonymus *and* Pinus mugo *are accompanied by the privet,* Ligustrum quihoui, *and the arching stems of* Rosa moyesii (*on the right*), Spiraea japonica *'Gold Mound' is in leaf and* Viburnum opulus *'Compactum' and* Weigela *'Florida Variegata' are in flower.* Gladiolus communis *subsp.* byzantinus *provides an element of brilliant colour after the tulips have departed. Siberian wallflowers, threaded among Goliath* poppies, *make pools of brightest orange. Foxgloves, bedded out the previous autumn, are just coming into flower. They will be replaced by dahlias and cannas by the turn of June–July.* Allium neapolitanum *is finishing its growing season by flowering, making a mass of white at the border's margin, with grey-green spikes of lyme grass just visible beyond. Tall* A. *'Purple Sensation', bedded out in the autumn, is making a show along with the big, mauve globes of* A. cristophii.

▶ **The second week of June**: *many alliums reach their peak now, notably* A. cristophii *whose globes dry in situ and form by self-sowing a running theme through much of the Long Border. Giant chives,* A. schoenoprasum *var.* sibiricum, *are still making a display in front of* Pinus mugo, *but must be cut to the ground before the seeds ripen. A bright green sedge,* Carex muskingumensis, *makes a good, long-lasting companion. The cardoons go from strength to strength, with their big, grey, deeply toothed leaves, behind the Goliath poppy's huge red blooms on 1.2m/4ft stems. The foxgloves here are the biennial* Digitalis purpurea, *but we vary the colour strain in different years. Aucubas,* Euonymus *and* Spiraea japonica *'Gold Mound' are still performing structural roles.*

▶ **The third week of July**: *the border goes full steam ahead.* Clematis *'Jackmanii Superba', growing up a pole that hoists it into the privet,* Ligustrum quihoui, *has been in flower since late June. We have left self-sown purple orach, teazels and verbascums as tall features, and some verbascums have also been added where necessary. Other yellow flowers include crocosmia, hemerocallis,* Inula magnifica *and* Silphium perfoliatum. *At the front of the border* Cosmos bipinnatus *'Sonata Pink', bedded out in May, is beginning to make a display next to* Carex muskingumensis. Geranium × riversleaianum *'Russell Prichard' is sprawling on to the path near the purple spikes of* Salvia nemorosa *'Ostfriesland'.* Helenium *'Moerheim Beauty' is making its first wave of bronze blossom. Phloxes and delphiniums, given support (discreet canes) in May, contribute to the scene. The tree-like* Dahlia imperialis *had a great presence in this year.*

▶ **The second week of August**: *three weeks later and the purple clematis is still flowering and the privet is in its prime with cascading panicles of white blossom. The cardoons at the back of the border are still looking good, flowering now with mauve thistle-heads that are popular with bees. Viburnum opulus 'Compactum', which had white lacecap flowers in May, now has dangling clusters of shining, red berries which last for a couple of months. Silphium perfoliatum has a long season, as does Cosmos bipinnatus 'Sonata Pink'. Crocosmias are invaluable late-flowering perennials. C. × crocosmiiflora 'Star of the East' in the foreground shows up against the dark-leaved Canna 'Mystique', the whole point of which is its upright, translucent foliage.*

▶ **Early September**: *summer bedding gives abundant colour, notably cannas and dahlias, as well as Silphium perfoliatum still going strong. Canna 'General Eisenhower' is in full bloom in the middle of the border and is just the right height not to conceal the virburnum's berries just behind it. Delphinium 'Mighty Atom', seen in flower in the July photograph, has had its flower spikes removed and its skeleton has been enlivened with the climbing annual Ipomoea lobata (syn. Mina lobata). We have removed the purple orach, Atriplex hortensis var. rubra, because although it is handsome as the seed heads are ripening in late summer, we want it out before the seeds are actually shed. You may also notice that we have weeded the gaps between the paving stones as this is one place where we don't want crack plants.*

▶ / ▶ ▶ **The beginning of October**: *the show goes on, and the border is as lively as it was in early July. Rosa moyesii and R. setipoda carry glamorous hips and Helenium 'Moerheim Beauty', dead-headed after its first crop of flowers, is almost as showy as it was in the summer. The cannas and Salvia coccinea 'Lady in Red' continue to give bright colour. Cosmos bipinnatus 'Sonata Pink' is as good as if not better than in September. Ipomoea lobata has engulfed the remains of the delphiniums with its clusters of tubular crimson-orange-and-yellow flowers on crimson stems, but is light enough to do no harm to the perennial. And still the aucubas, Euonymus fortunei 'Silver Queen', Pinus mugo and Libertia peregrinans provide the border's anchors, with cardoons, Carex muskingumensis and Spiraea japonica 'Gold Mound' performing similarly important roles.*

A succession planting beneath Prunus tenella, a dwarf almond of suckering habit.

▲ **In February** the substantial snowdrop Galanthus 'S. Arnott' flowers with self-sowing Crocus tommasinianus beneath the naked twigs of the almond. The snowdrop rapidly multiplies by division.

▶ **In late April** exactly the same area with wreaths of pink blossom clothing the almond, which will afterwards be pruned by cutting its stems to within inches of the ground. The underplanting is now dominated by the rather late-flowering, clear lemon yellow Cyclamineus daffodil, Narcissus 'Hawera'. Its perianth segments are turned back, as is characteristic in this group.

GOOD GARDENING

Successions are my main concern, but they are linked to other aspects of good gardening and must work hand in hand with them. When you have a new plant, you must think first of where it is likely to succeed. Will the soil that is to receive it be congenial? If not, make it so. Are the weeds in this area healthy? If not, there is something wrong that needs to be remedied. If weeds will not thrive, how can other plants be expected to?

Is soil acidity likely to be a problem or is your new plant pretty tolerant about this, as far as you know? I believe in working with the acidity or otherwise that is natural to your soil. Let someone else grow the rhododendrons, azaleas and camellias that you could only provide for with a specially made bed, having imported acid soil.

Will your plant prefer to be in full sun, or would it like some shade in the heat of the day? One of the trickiest situations is where trees overhang the planting area, because where there are branches there'll be greedy roots beneath. To cut the branches back will help, but their roots will still be active. On the other hand (and here our subject of successions creeps in), most trees lose their leaves in winter, which allows light to reach the ground beneath them. You must take advantage of this situation with plants which do most

of their growing during the short days, when deciduous trees are leafless. The shadows from houses are entirely predictable; root-free, but the sun's position and altitude will largely dictate your choice of plants.

You must consider exposure and whether your plant will tolerate much wind or, indeed, the high-speed draughts that the close presence of buildings often generates. And you'll often find that when wind hits a building, its speed is increased in the opposite direction on bouncing off it. So your plantings will lean away from the building rather than towards it. This can be an advantage when trees are in question. They will be less likely to fall on your house.

In normal situations soft-textured plants will lean away from the direction of the wind. In our climate this has repercussions that need to be taken into account. Our strongest winds tend to come from the southwest. But, given the choice, we will site our borders where they face towards the south and receive plenty of sunshine. Your soft-textured plants will be blown away from your viewpoint at the border's front (assuming this is a one-sided border). One that occurs to me is the grass *Miscanthus sinensis* 'Silberfeder' (Silver Feather), which flowers attractively in September. It is self-supporting but still, because of its flexible stems,

The giant fennel, Ferula communis, *builds up slowly from its January start but doesn't reach its eventual size for months, thus offering space for temporary displays.*

▲ **In April** *giant fennel foliage, consisting of innumerable, thread-fine divisions, forms an undulating background for tall, late-flowering, red tulips, here Tulipa 'Halcro'. Leaf growth continues until May–June, when the fennel's inflorescence develops with startling rapidity.*

▶ **In June** *Ferula communis reaches its peak by running up to 2.5m/8ft or more, carrying corymbs of yellow-green blossom. As they fade, the plant quickly dies away completely until the following January. We interplant with annuals, such as Cosmos and Tagetes, sown in early May to flower in late summer and autumn. Seed of the fennel should be sown fresh.*

is looking the wrong way. This can be corrected, with careful, invisible staking, and Fergus does it, but you need to know how. Or else to avoid this kind of plant!

You also need to bear in mind that many flowers will face towards the sun, even moving around as they follow the sun's path. Sunflowers and other members of their family are typical. Your own viewpoints should take advantage of this. For example, if you have double borders running east and west, the plants on the north side will tend to look towards the south and your view of them will be good. On the south side, however, these sun-facing flowers will be looking away from you and will give you a poor view. They should not, therefore, replicate those used on the north side but should be of a kind that takes little notice of light direction – hollyhocks, for instance, or delphiniums. And if you live in the southern hemisphere, you'll have to turn my advice upside down.

At the same time as ensuring, so far as you can, that your new plant will grow happily, you must think about its neighbours. How will it look in their company? This is very important. Create your picture first and then think about extending the season. You can

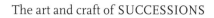

either alter the neighbours to suit your plant's proximity or you can make sure that your new-comer will go well with the plants that are already there. Will it, or do you want it to coincide in its top performance with its neighbours'? You need to get your sequences right. When not flowering – or doing whatever its principal function is expected to be – will it contribute to the gaiety of nations in other ways? Or will it leave a staring blank? If a blank, there'll be ways of coping with that, too. It won't be the end of the world.

A HIGH POINT

It is easiest to succeed in our object by focusing on a high point in the year, when everything visible is contributing towards perfection. In the cool-temperate climate where I live, in southeast England, July is the month when most plants, whether wild or cultivated, are geared to flowering. Gertrude Jekyll, our greatest national gardener a century ago, preferred to focus on August. But you may be away from home in August and prefer to concentrate your efforts on a spring or early-summer season. After our high point, we don't want our borders to run out of steam as autumn approaches, however good the skeletons may be on the winter scene. Keep an eye on the balance between colours. A feeling of freshness can be sustained well into October, given a bit of shuffling around with the contents.

Whenever your climax may be, you can endlessly extend, by the art and craft of successions, your border's interest and display at either end, but still without detracting from its chosen climax. There is a host of devices for achieving this ambition.

Using your eyes is critical and you need to study your border year-round, pretty well every day in fact, ever criticising, ever assessing and working out how things might be done better. In winter it is worth looking at spaces and thinking whether they are necessary. My mother used to plant what she called 'daddy's little surprises', to which she would lead my father, freezing in front of them till his mind concentrated on what was there that she wanted him to notice. Usually it was snowdrops, tucked into a gap the previous year and now in flower. Most of those snowdrop-filled gaps have now been overgrown by the hedge behind them, but some remain. Besides which, if you choose fertile snowdrops, they'll self-sow and spread themselves into the spaces that they can find.

A space is an opportunity and spaces can develop at times of year other than winter. Be ready to pounce on them. The giant fennel, *Ferula communis* (this is not the one you eat), is a classic

Rodgersia pinnata
'Maurice Mason' is a choice
plant for moist, partially
shaded positions. We grow
it in the Barn Garden in a
north-facing bed with heavy
soil, backed by a retaining
wall and yew hedge, where
snowdrops and other early
bulbs make a January
display.

▲ **In May** the rodgersia's
flower buds and rich bronze-
purple leaves are enlivened
by the globe heads of Allium
hollandicum 'Purple
Sensation'.

▲ ▶ **By mid June** the
rodgersia's thick-textured
leaves have turned green
and expanded to display
the rough, heavily veined
surface. The flower stems
have almost reached full
height (1m/3ft) and
panicles of rich pink flowers
are about to open. I used
to have glaucous hostas in
front but they were martyrs
to slugs and snails and their
foliage became a reproach
early in the season. Not so
the rodgersias: pests do not
attack them and the hand-
some, palmate leaves are a
perennial asset. The golden
colouring of Carex elata
'Aurea' (in the foreground)
is at its peak now. Behind
the rodgersia a few pale-
green heads remain on

example. It starts to grow as early as January, but takes months to
achieve its eventual size. For spring, then, you can fill in with tulips
around it. The fennel flowers in June and then dies off quickly,
so as to become invisible (although if you acquire a perennial
kind, it will live indefinitely). It aestivates; takes a summer siesta.
So around it, to perform from midsummer onwards, you plant
anything temporary that's handy and fairly quick off the mark.
It might be cosmos or marigolds. After which the cycle starts all
over again.

BETTER PLANTS

To help us in our borders, we want to think of plants having
a number of assets, perhaps handsome flowers, foliage and attractive seed heads. We'll not be able to fill our spaces with such paragons, but they do exist. And we are always vigilant not just for good
plants but for better plants. You must not be afraid of change. On
the other hand, you must not get so fidgety that you don't give your
new plants time to settle down and prove themselves before you
move them again. Every plant is looked at critically, over a long
period. We may decide, within a year, that it could be improved

May-flowering Euphorbia palustris. *Another good companion, also relishing good moisture-retaining soil, is a herbaceous member of the ivy family,* Aralia cachemirica, *with boldly pinnate leaves still coming on; its compound umbels of blossom later in the summer are followed by black-purple fruits. Right at the back the Hybrid Musk rose 'Cornelia' is in its first flush of blossom. I cannot remember why or when I put it here in partial shade, but it has proved itself over many years and has a second flowering.*

▲ ▶ **Towards the end of July** *the leaves of* Rodgersia pinnata 'Maurice Mason' *are beginning to acquire coppery tones and the colour of the flowers has deepened as it runs imperceptibly to seed. The inflorescence is still beautiful as the season progresses, remaining in perfect condition into October. Such long-season paragons are what we need for succession plantings.*

on, or it may take five years or more. Our yardstick is not just how the plant behaves with us but how it looks in other gardens and quite frequently how similar but slightly different plants may have more desirable qualities than our own.

Plants with a long season are a great help and you will be sharp in finding them. Sometimes young plants will give you twice the length of performance time that old ones can. My classic example here is *Anthemis tinctoria* in any of its cultivated forms. Young stock, say from basal cuttings taken in February from the cushion of young shoots with which it overwinters, will start flowering in early July and will go right on without pause for four months. They'll be half the inconvenient height of old stock and all they'll ask of you, besides good soil and a sunny position, is one deadheading. Old stock will give a single bout of flowering in early summer and will then just look horrible with mildew. More and more, gardeners are tending to treat perennials as biennials, simply because young stock is so much more productive and healthier than old.

You must make sure you are growing your plants well and thereby getting the best response from them. There is a bed of

▲ Cyclamen hederifolium displays its foliage all through the winter at the foot of deciduous shrubs, here Weigela 'Florida Variegata', and can be seen right across the deep, one-sided Long Border. The flowers in August will be concealed.

▼ The narrow-leaved species tulip, Tulipa linifolia, which grows to

a mere 15cm/6in tall but opens wide and brilliantly in spring sunshine, can be left in situ from year to year. We have planted the horned poppy, Glaucium flavum f. fulvum, around and between the bulbs. We grow a fresh batch of poppy seedlings every year for the foliage that forms a basal rosette and is felted grey, with sinuous margins.

cannas at Wisley, hardy because against a south-facing greenhouse, but horribly congested. This not only shortens their flowering season but also reduces the quality of the flowers and foliage. (Probably this will have changed by the time you get there.) Leave them there all winter by all means if, climatically, you can get away with it, but lift, split and replant them in rejuvenated soil as they begin to show renewed signs of life the next spring.

In looking for the best, remember that the Royal Horticultural Society (RHS) tries to help and to guide with its Award of Garden Merit (AGM), which is signalled as such in the *RHS Plant Finder* (well worth its purchase price on each of its annual appearances). This award is made on practical judgements of the growing plant, not just cut stems. And it is made by a practical team of experts, both amateur and professional, with many areas of expertise. The award is a guide only, when all is said. By choosing an AGM plant you give yourself, I should say, a 60:40 chance of having done the sensible thing. Better than a blind stab in the dark.

In succession plantings the weak points inherent in nearly all types of plant are catered for by the strengths of their neighbours. Even so, good management is essential. Staking and dead-heading must be kept up to date, but unobtrusively. The visitor doesn't want to be made aware of mechanics, if they can be performed discreetly, which they usually can.

MULTI-LAYERED BORDERS

We are adding to our borders layer upon layer, all the time. Subtracting, too. Anchor plants to the left include tall cardoons, *Cynara cardunculus*, which look handsome for foliage, flowers and seed heads through most of the year; and a pair of seedling *Eucalyptus gunnii*, grown for their glaucous juvenile foliage and cut hard back each spring, to keep them in this juvenile state. They need replacing every few years.

In front is the poppy generally known as *Papaver bracteatum* 'Goliath' (the *RHS Plant Finder* would have us call it *P. orientale* Goliath Group). It has strong, sturdy stems (though still in need of staking) to 1m/3ft or more and large, rich crimson, dark-centred flowers. The clumps are fairly widely spaced (nearly 1m/3ft), but not so widely as to leave gaps between them when in flower, in May–June. The poppies have no objection to being cut right down to the ground after flowering, that is before mid June, so you can leave large enough gaps between their clumps to bed out some-thing like *Dianthus* that will take over for the summer.

In spring there are tulips between poppy clumps. We run quantities of tulips along the border's entire length. They are a principal theme from March to May. To right, *Allium giganteum* and a quickly increasing hybrid called 'Globemaster'. Behind is a key shrub, *Viburnum opulus* 'Compactum'. It can easily be kept to 2m/6ft by pruning out its flowered wood, leaving just unflowered. It is deciduous and flowers in late May like a lacecap hydrangea, that is with an outer ring of largish, sterile, white florets and an inner disc of small, fertile, white ones. After flowering it quite quickly sets bunches of shiny, translucent, red berries. These are already ripe in August and for some reason the birds never touch them, so they hang on for a couple of months. This viburnum suckers mildly and at its base are a number of small, self-appointed plants: *Allium cristophii*, a great self-sower, primroses, *Cyclamen hederifolium* (invaluable for its marbled foliage) and forget-me-nots (*Myosotis*), these last comprising another theme that runs right through the border, being topped up from other parts of the garden, where there are gaps.

To left, a shrub rose given by her daughter-in-law to my mother in the 1930s: 'Perle d'Or', which is a miniature Hybrid Tea rose like 'Cécile Brünner' but buff, not pink. It makes quite a large bush. This has similar plants at its base to those harboured

▼ *The creamy white tulip 'Françoise' and self-sowing primroses bridge the period when* Papaver orientale Goliath Group *is gathering strength. The bare stems of* Rosa setipoda *and the jagged, grey-green leaves of cardoon,* Cynara cardunculus, *can be seen behind.*

Oriental poppies are far easier to deal with in successions than lupins, say, which refuse to go away (*see pages 96–7*). The poppies have no objection to being cut right down to the ground after flowering, that is before mid June, so you can leave large enough gaps between their clumps to bed out something that will take over for the rest of the summer.

▲ **In May–June** *Papaver orientale Goliath Group* is in flower at the same time as the *Guelder rose,* Viburnum opulus '*Compactum',* and Rosa setipoda.

▶ **Early August** *and* Canna '*General Eisenhower',* planted in the gaps left by the Goliath poppies, is showing great style. This canna is of medium height, thereby not concealing the display of fruit on Viburnum opulus '*Compactum'* behind. The canna on the left, not in flower, is the taller C. indica '*Purpurea'.* At top left are the long hairy hips of Rosa setipoda. The aggressive blue lyme grass, Leymus arenarius, dug up every spring and replanted as a demure clump, is a focal point, with satellites on both sides, in this case Salvia coccinea '*Lady in Red'.*

by the viburnum, and so does yet another rose, left again, *Rosa setipoda,* which I struck from a cutting out of my friend Alan Roger's garden in West Ross-shire. Its flower buds and later its fruits are covered in bristles. The single flowers are pink – white at the centre; the hips are orange. I prune it by removing flowered branches, in winter, and leaving young, unflowered, unbranched shoots entirely intact (no tipping, please).

The Goliath poppies, when cut to the ground in June, are interplanted with a red canna, 'General Eisenhower'. I wanted a red canna in this position but not so tall as to conceal the viburnum behind it. This canna is just right. It is treated much like a dahlia, the tuberous rhizomes being stored, once frosted, in old wooden wine crates, treated against rotting. They go into old potting soil (watered perhaps once every two or three weeks, to prevent shrivelling) and kept in a dark, cool cellar. When they show signs of activity in spring, the boxes are moved to a deep cold frame with solid walls and kept closed till the cannas are well established. They are hardened off and planted out in June, being split then if the clumps have grown too large.

In front of all these and next to the path margin is one clump (another key plant) of the blue-leaved grass, a native and virtually a giant couch, *Leymus arenarius*. To control its invasive habits, Fergus has to replant it every spring, tracing and removing all the long underground runners made the previous year. We plant a range of vividly flowering bedding either side of it – such as *Dianthus* 'Ideal Crimson' and 'Ideal Scarlet', followed by *Salvia coccinea* 'Lady in Red'. To right but still on the border's margin, *Santolina pinnata* subsp. *neapolitana,* which is cut hard back every spring but then makes a neat hummock of grey during the summer. It does the job of concealing the dying leaves of the alliums behind it because, as is the way with many alliums, their leaves wither before they have flowered.

To right of these, a group of early July-flowering delphiniums, one called 'Mighty Atom', with mauve flowers and of only moderate height. When this has flowered, the flowering stems are removed to just above its leaves and it is soon completely obliterated by a climbing annual, *Mina* (correctly *Ipomoea*) *lobata*, in yellow and red.

So you see that this type of gardening is quite complex but of immense interest and we are learning all the time. 'It's all a lot of work,' did I hear someone moaning? Of course it is, but the rewards are there and immensely satisfying, even if you're the only one who fully appreciates the effort expended to achieve them.

Layered planting plans

We are adding to our borders layer upon layer in every season. Subtracting, too. This all takes time and cannot easily be shown on paper as it is so fluid and includes over-lapping, but Fergus has made the attempt. This 9m/30ft section is taken from the middle of the Long Border, which, you remember, is 4.5m/15ft deep and south-west facing. It is backed by a tall yew hedge and fronted by a flagstone path.

Key to planting plans

First layer

▢	*Papaver orientale* Goliath Group
G	*Geranium* 'Ann Folkard'
R	*Rosa* 'Perle d'Or'
Sa	*Salvia nemorosa* 'Ostfriesland' (East Friesland)
S	*Santolina pinnata* subsp. *neapolitana*

Second layer

 Tulipa

Hyacinthus orientalis 'King of the Blues'

Allium cristophii

Allium giganteum

Camassia leichtlinii subsp. *suksdorfii* 'Electra'

Cyclamen hederifolium

Third layer

Myosotis sylvatica

Viola odorata

Primula vulgaris

Fourth layer

Ammi majus

Dianthus 'Ideal Crimson'

Dianthus 'Ideal Violet'

Fifth layer

Canna × *ehemanii*

Canna 'General Eisenhower'

Salvia coccinea 'Lady in Red'

Ipomoea lobata (syn. *Mina lobata*)

▶ Anchor plants and key perennials, the foundations on which we build, appear in each plan, but note the succession of interest in the spaces occupied by clumps of Papaver orientale Goliath Group. The emerging foliage looks good with early bulbs, it flowers from May to June and is cut right down after flowering to make way for summer bedding.
▲ Viburnum opulus 'Compactum' is a valuable shrub, easily kept to 2m/6ft by pruning.

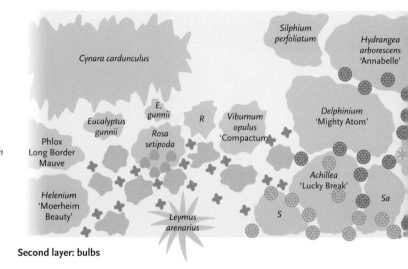

First layer: anchor plants and key perennials

▶ The Long Border is laced with bulbs that add interest from spring and into autumn with allium seed heads.

▲ We ring the changes with tulips, here the orange, Lily-flowered Tulipa 'Ballerina' among forget-me-nots, Myosotis.

Second layer: bulbs

▶ Self-sowers add an element of spontaneity. We give myosotis a helping hand by thinning seedlings where they are too dense, or too few, by adding from elsewhere in the garden.

▲ The wild primrose, Primula vulgaris, is an opportunist that puts itself beneath deciduous shrubs.

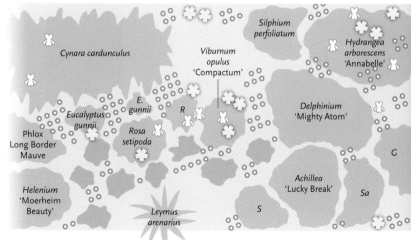

Third layer: self-sowers

▶ Bedding makes colour possible from spring to autumn. We pounce on gaps to fit in bedding, such as tall Ammi majus at the back and short dianthus at the front.

▲ Ammi majus is planted out in early April and by May the stems have risen to 2m/6ft, topped with clouds of white flowers.

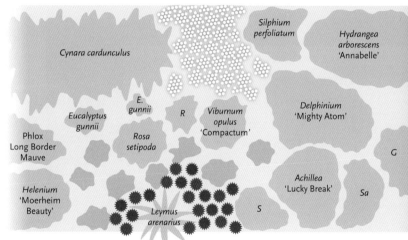

Fourth layer: spring/early-summer bedding

▶ We sweep aside early bedding plants once they finish flowering and replace them with late-summer annuals and tender perennials. Here tall cannas have replaced the ammi and Salvia coccinea 'Lady in Red' takes the place of the dianthus. These keep the show going into October.

▲ Canna 'General Eisenhower' in the spaces between the Goliath poppies, now dormant.

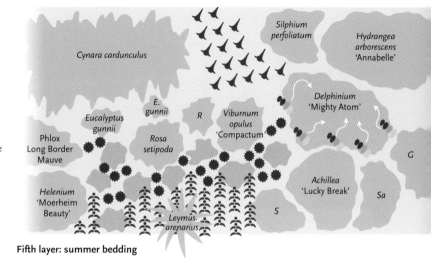

Fifth layer: summer bedding

29

ANCHOR PLANTS
the core necessity

Structural plants are essential in any kind of planting, large-scale or small. They provide the feel of continuity and the core to achieving a long-season effect.

◀ Although the hardiness of Melianthus major *arouses anxiety in its proud owner, my colony has been with me for more than fifty years. Its roots are heavily protected in winter with a mulch of dead ferns and bracken. The next season's young shoots appear quite late and the large, deeply toothed leaves are at their best in autumn, making three-dimensional sculptures in low sunlight, and generally remaining in good condition through to December.*

Foliage is the dominant characteristic of plants that give body to a planting. That doesn't rule out flowers, but flowers are not the essence of the contribution that anchor plants make to successions. Non-flowering plants are important for many reasons. Foliage makes a border more digestible. If you focus on flowers only, the impact hits your eyes so that they hurt. Foliage calms and has a unifying effect. It also prolongs a border's season so that it may well be year-round.

Leaves have great advantages. They are many-faceted, even more so than flowers. The larger ones create a sculptural effect and are inclined to be bolder than most flowers and for a longer period. Leaves have a great range of shapes as well as colours and textures and, whatever their size, they can be bold. That applies to bamboos and grasses, ferns and many perennials. There are also tender bedding plants with long-season foliage – cannas, castor oil plants, *Tetrapanax, Eupatorium capillifolium* and others on which I write later.

Leaves may be light-reflecting and glossy and aware of the state of the sky at any one time and certainly of sunshine striking them. Glossy leaves will also bring light into shady places. No corner of your garden, even where the side of buildings hems you in, need be dark or dismal. By contrast, leaves may be felted and light-absorbing and of velvety texture. They invite you to grasp them

between fingers and thumb. Or prickly; the very hostility with which they confront you has its own appeal. The pads of certain cacti may be far from cuddly, but they are often arranged on different planes, playing tricks with light and shade and thereby enhancing a feeling of depth and a heightened awareness of the third dimension.

Because of their 'look-at-me' element, I generally, in my own garden setting, prefer large-leaved plants to small. Gardens are, after all, for display. If leaves are tiny, as with heathers, the plant must fall back on colour for the effect it achieves. On the other hand, many colourful-foliage heathers have been bred and can give you sustenance year-round, the colours themselves changing with the season. And the plants will tend to be tougher than those which are large-leaved.

With some of us, variegated-leaved plants have great appeal. Fine, but don't grow many of them all together. They need more restful, less busy surroundings to set them off.

TREES IN YOUR BORDERS

For ease of explanation, I categorize the different plants that give us structure, starting with trees. These are manipulated or not, according to scale. The size of the trees you can include in your borders also depends on the scale. If they are naturally slow-growing – and slow growers generally develop the most character – they will take a long time to become trees and will require no pruning at all. *Cornus alternifolia* 'Argentea' is like that. It rises slowly in horizontal layers, sometimes taking two or three years to make up its mind to grow the next layer. In the summer it is light and airy, with white-variegated foliage. When that is shed, you can enjoy its horizontal branch structure and you will notice how raindrops remain suspended on it, each catching the light and glistening. Who has need of flowers when there is such a paragon as this?

The evergreen *Daphniphyllum himalaense* subsp. *macropodum* is another slow grower. It follows the general rule that evergreens are less hardy than deciduous trees and shrubs, so you give it a bit of shelter. The more you see of this tree, the more you realize there is to see. Superficially its elliptical leaves, borne in rotate clusters, look like a rhododendron's, but they are not a bit. The undersides are smooth and silvery, while the leaf stalks, in winter, change to bright pink. Its 'look-at-me' qualities ensure that nobody ever misses it, whether standing close or as far away as sight lines

▲ *Foliage makes a difference on a small scale as well as a large. The shaded corner of a bed has an interweaving of* Polystichum setiferum *'Pulcherrimum Bevis',* Asarum europaeum, *with shiny leaves that reflect any light that's going, and the rosette-forming spurge,* Euphorbia amygdaloides var. robbiae, *which has a rather running habit, so that you need to act as referee to ensure that it doesn't muscle out the others. These all suit a fairly heavily shaded space and provide a little stab of pleasure when I pass them.*

▼ Daphniphyllum himalaense *subsp.* macropodum *is a distinguished-looking evergreen of surprising hardiness. It stands out in the landscape as well as being fascinating at close quarters. In a good strain, the leaf stalks assume a bright pink colouring through the winter months.*

▲ Cornus alternifolia 'Argentea' is possibly the most rewarding shrub in my garden the whole year round. It is deciduous but provides just as much enjoyment when bare and raindrops catch the light on its horizontal branches as when it is fully clothed with small, white-margined leaves. It rises slowly up to 4.5m/15ft over a long period of years. We allow forget-me-nots and yellow Welsh poppies to self-sow underneath. If you do not want tiered branches right down to ground level, you can remove the lowest and plant shade-tolerant perennials, such as the yellow-flowered Erythronium tuolumnense for April–May effect or Arisaema consanguineum for a summer display. This arisaema has a mildly running rootstock and will build up to a colony. The fascinating structure of its leaves is its principal appeal.

allow. Close, you will appreciate that it is hung, just behind the leaves, with clusters of small, black, grape-like berries. We rarely prune it, but if some of its branches do begin to look a bit stemmy, you can cut them back and it will willingly 'break' from old wood.

A good Japanese maple, did you want? Fergus and I would wholeheartedly recommend *Acer palmatum* 'Sango-kaku' (alias 'Senkaki'). A small tree, in time, with brilliant green foliage in spring, the leaves quite small. Then prolonged autumn colour, yellow gradually deepening to gold. Finally, after leaf-fall, young twigs that are a really lively pink. But the first time I tried it, in my mixed border, it simply turned up its toes. I think conditions must have been too rich. Eventually it settled down in a comparatively poor piece of ground, acid, of course (none of these maples will put up with lime), and it gives us prolonged pleasure for a large part of the year. *Acer palmatum* 'Shishigashira' is not everyone's idea of the way a Japanese maple should look but its strong personality struck me from the first time I clapped eyes on it. I wanted it and I have it, doing a wonderful anchoring job, in the middle of a fluctuating melée of mixed border contents. Its upright habit is chunky and dense without being coarse. Its smallish

▲ Among the popular Japanese maples derived from Acer palmatum, 'Shishigashira' has an unusually chunky habit, which enables it to be used in a border as a firm anchor for less permanent features. Its summer dress (left) is unusually dark green and lasts into November when it changes quite suddenly into burnished bronze (centre) before shedding. When bare in winter (right), it is still fascinating in the varied colouring of the young twigs; these are glaucous but tipped with red which are next year's dormant buds. The interior takes on a greenish patina.

leaves settle down to an unusually deep green and give a feeling of richness in late summer and early autumn, when much else is looking tired. Eventually the colour changes to burnished bronze, before shedding; that is not till November. Its winter aspect is scarcely less arresting. Next year's leaf buds are red but the web of young shoots behind them is overlaid by a soft grey bloom. Behind this, the older stems are olive green. Overall there is a purposeful concentration that inspires confidence.

There are other trees, excellent for mixed-border inclusion, whose size does need controlling; that is, whose growth needs shortening. Dickson's golden elm, *Ulmus glabra* 'Dampieri Aurea', is one such. On its young shoots, the gold-green leaves are arranged closely in two ranks and they overlap like feathers on a bird's wing. We prune ours over every other year, both so as to encourage plenty of young growth and to contain its loftiness to no higher than our tallest member of staff can reach from a ladder leaning against the tree's framework (Health & Safety authorities, please don't read). The whole tree, from a distance, shines like a beacon. It could be the continuation of the biennial mullein, *Verbascum olympicum*, which has similar upwards-reaching aspirations from a lower level.

Many *Salix*, the willows, lend themselves admirably to cutting

back, usually termed pollarding in their case. So, in front of the elm I have a group of three *Salix alba* var. *sericea*, which is a particularly pale, silvery variant of our native white willow, *S. alba*.

One of my Long Border's most striking ingredients is a tall holly, lightly clipped with secateurs to make a slender cone at one end and at the back of the border, which is one-sided with yew hedging for a background. This is *Ilex × altaclerensis* 'Golden King', almost prickle-free (which makes for painless hand-weeding around it) and variegated with a yellow margin to a green centre.

There are some trees whose character is entirely changed by manipulation, which entails pruning back hard into old wood. They too are grist to our mixed-border mill. The tree of heaven, *Ailanthus altissima*, is most familiar in London and similar rather smoke-laden industrial centres as a tolerator of those conditions. But if you grow it from seed and, when the seedling is well established, make a practice of cutting it back each winter, almost to the ground, it will make a splendid foliage plant. Restrict its growth to one shoot and it will put on 4.5m/15ft annually, its pinnate leaves each more than 1m/3ft long. Although entirely hardy, this will create a thoroughly exotic effect. *Paulownia tomentosa* and *Catalpa bignonioides* respond in the same way, the latter particularly effective in the golden-leaved *C.b.* 'Aurea', which is immensely expensive because it has to be grafted on to plain-leaved seedlings and only the Dutch are doing it.

Other trees that have to be grafted are many deciduous variegated kinds, like the white-variegated sweet chestnut, *Castanea sativa* 'Albomarginata', and the even more beautiful but rarer golden-variegated *C. s.* 'Variegata'.

▶ Ilex × altaclerensis *'Golden King' is one of the most eye-catching features in the Long Border. It is at the back and at the top in the angle of two yew hedges. Despite its name, this holly is a female and easily pollinated by surrounding wildings which are abundant. It ripens long-lasting berries in most years and can be used on the Christmas pudding.*

◀ *Pinus mugo is a great anchor plant near the corner where a path bisects the Long Border.*

In late April (*top*), *gaps between the pine's branches were planted with the striking red tulip 'Red Matador', having wonderfully marked yet murky-coloured centres on opening wide, and now that that is no longer on offer we are happy with the similar 'Apeldoorn'. In front of the pine is spiky Libertia* peregrinans, *with the bronze colouring so typical of much of New Zealand's flora.*

In mid August (*below far left*), *self-sown nasturtiums are scrambling over the pine and in this year we planted Zinnia 'Profusion Orange' between it and a permanent planting of giant chives.*

In the early October scene (*below left*), *the backdrop of a favourite ornamental grass, Miscanthus sinensis 'Silberfeder' (Silver Feather), is in full flower and the nasturtiums are still going strong, with dark purple cannas behind. The corner piece of* Yucca gloriosa *'Variegata' makes an end stop.*

In the second week in November (*below*), *the yucca on the corner looks almost exactly the same as it has all year, as does the pine. (The photograph on page 10 shows this scene from a wider angle.) The colour of the* Miscanthus *bleaches as the stems die, but the shape of the plant, if we are spared fierce winds, continues to be a feature till December or even later. With time, Miscanthus clumps increase unduly and we exercise girth control by chopping around the circumference on an annual basis.*

ANCHORING EVERGREEN SHRUBS

When we turn to shrubs, we may well be bewildered by the huge numbers available, so it is up to us to do the sorting and winnowing. Many are dull or coarse; conifers like Leyland cypress, for instance. Be wary of which conifers you choose.

The only conifer in my Long Border is *Pinus mugo*, which I grew from seed collected in the Carpathians. It is a 1m/3ft-tall bush which I keep to that height by pinching its young shoots each spring back by half. It has a sprawling habit, as in nature, where it grows near the tree line, and between its arms there are tulips in spring, while self-sown nasturtiums investigate in summer.

When writing of trees, I mentioned the holly, *Ilex* 'Golden King' as being a year-round primadonna in my Long Border. An anchoring shrub of equal significance at the 1.2m/4ft level is *Euonymus fortunei* 'Silver Queen'. The genuine article is exceedingly slow-growing. I planted it about 1m/3ft back from the path margin and it took many years to reach forwards to the path itself. But it has all the advantages of a slow, yet healthy grower, developing a presence which cannot be matched by the quicker-growing substitutes, like *E. f.* 'Emerald Gaiety' and 'Emerald 'n' Gold', which have been developed for the impatient gardener (and which are good in their way). 'Silver Queen' has a broad band of variegation on its margin, which is pale yellow when young, in spring, but matures to silver. Although devoid of chlorophyll (so far as I can tell), it never scorches, though the shrub is in full sun. Occasionally a small branch reverts to plain green, immediately showing its true character by setting typical spindle-berry fruit. Of course, I cut this out. The shrub is planted around with a range of shrubs and plants of comparatively makeshift habit, but the euonymus effortlessly queens them all.

Another evergreen is the laurel, *Prunus laurocerasus* 'Otto Luyken', with glossy, light-reflecting foliage. It is popular and you might dismissively refer to it, as one friend did, as motorway stuff. This laurel is neat and compact in habit and I keep it, with secateurs (not shears, which cut ugly gashes across the leaves), to a height of about 2m/6ft. Although principally a foliage plant, it flowers too, not once but (in the south of England at least) twice, being given a dead-heading in between. The flowers, in clustered spikelets, are white and fragrant (a bit sickly, but I like it). It is a year-round performer, but with a floral bonus. Half the point of it is its neighbour, *Thuja occidentalis* 'Rheingold', which makes a broad cone of similar height to the laurel's. Its colour changes with the seasons, being sometimes such a dark brown in winter that you might

think it was dying. Far from it. The two shrubs, side by side by a path edge, are a joy.

A garden remaining in the same family's hands for a century slowly evolves. You can see it as a story of successions on an extended time scale. Our Barn Garden surrounding the Sunk Garden (octagonal pool in centre) is an enclosed area that demands four semi-formal features at the corners to define its squarish shape. My father planted *Yucca gloriosa*, surrounded by the spears of bearded iris leaves. Yuccas are excellent for this purpose in many ways, but this one has stiff, sharp leaf points which my mother feared would gouge out a child's or a dog's eye. So when my father died, in 1933, she replaced the yuccas with an ornamental flowering crab, *Malus sargentii*, which she had admired in flower at a Chelsea Flower Show. It was quite unsuitable for the position, making large, spreading bushes of no character.

So when I got my claws into the garden, I decided to replace the crabs with four of the evergreen *Osmanthus delavayi*. On the whole, I think the choice, made in 1956, has worked well enough. The bushes are clipped over annually in late April, immediately after flowering, to form globes. The clipping stimulates them to make quite long young shoots during the ensuing growing season and it is along these that they flower, in March–April, with clusters of little, tubular, white, heavily scented flowers in the axil of every leaf.

The leaves of *Osmanthus delavayi* are small and unimportant-

In January *the garden's bones are exposed, revealing the underlying geometry. Outstanding in the mist are anchoring grasses:* Calamagrostis × acutiflora *'Karl Foerster' (on the left), then the dwarf pampas,* Cortaderia selloana *'Pumila', and to the right of that a cultivar of* Miscanthus sinensis. *But they are becoming scruffy and we shall cut them down before the month is out.*

▶ **In April** *anchor plants and hedges are a strong backdrop for massed tulips.* Osmanthus delavayi *is in flower; the bushes will have their annual clip later in the month, immediately after flowering, which will restore their globe shapes. In the background are* Prunus laurocerasus *'Latifolia' and, to its right, our old friend* Acer palmatum *'Shishigashira'. The bush cherry,* Prunus glandulosa *'Alba Plena', is wreathed with double white pompoms along all the previous year's young shoots. I prune it hard after flowering to encourage plenty of new growth. Pots with ornamental contents are stood around, one large group being of special importance, particularly when it included* Furcraea longaeva *with a 2.5m/8ft inflorescence that heralded its demise.*

▶ **July abundance** *includes quite a free-for-all growth of vegetation over much of the Sunk Garden floor. The young burrs on* Acaena novae-zelandiae *turn brilliant carmine and contrast with the yellow of self-introduced bird's-foot trefoil,* Lotus corniculatus. Dactylorhiza fuchsii *have sown themselves into the cracks among the mat formers. Very tall are self-sown teazels and evening primroses,* Oenothera glazioviana. *We plunge water-loving features, such as the pale yellow Argentinean* Canna glauca, *in the pool to add to the summer and autumn display.*

▶▶ **By September** *(overleaf), even when they are engulfed by vegetation, anchor plants still have an important role.*

▶ **Early October** *and the scene is as colourful as ever, the crimson berries on* Cotoneaster horizontalis *even more eye-catching than bright orange-flowered 'geraniums'. The cotoneaster is one of our most valued anchor plants, here projecting in big brackets from the top of retaining walls. Its fishbone structure looks good at every season of the year and foliage is retained from February to December. Beyond the yew hedge is* Crataegus persimilis *'Prunifolia', which has dark red haws, and colours up its foliage if the crop of berries is not too exhausting.* Osmanthus delavayi *will remain important as a dark green globe until the cycle begins again.*

looking, but the bushes make an excellent background to large-leaved plants, sited in front of them, notably *Melianthus major*. Another shrub (I have several, because it self-sows) that also has small leaves but balances well with the *Osmanthus* is the New Zealander, *Olearia solandri*. This grows into a large yet not domineering shrub and is of what I consider typical New Zealand colouring, a kind of living greeny-brown. It is not a shrub that attracts the public's attention, but it certainly does mine, being scented on the air, year-round, of heliotrope.

With some shrubs, you have little idea at the time of planting how they will behave over the years, but you adapt. I have a Jerusalem sage, *Phlomis fruticosa*, whose date of acquisition (I pinched it) I can remember because I was working during my vacation from Wye College (studying horticulture) at the old and soon-to-be-defunct nursery of Wallace, The Old Gardens, Tunbridge Wells, Kent. It was in 1950. Mine is an excellent form of the species, as Rowland Jackman remarked when he paid me a visit, with incurved leaves so that you can see both surfaces. It flowers for quite a long spell, late June to July, and the hooded flowers (for it is a labiate, now *Lamiaceae*) are dusky yellow and borne in whorls in two or three terminal tiers. When you dead-head them, you are liable to get a painful paroxism of hay fever, unless the bush is wet at the time, but some people are totally unaffected.

The main point is that *Phlomis fruticosa* is never shabby and never has an off-season. In the course of years it has become incredibly rangy, so that other plants, like border phloxes in summer and snowdrops in winter, have established between its arms. It has amazing character.

I have had the same colony of *Melianthus major* for half a century now, so it is well established and, having brought it in, I will dwell on it awhile, as it plays such a vital role at Dixter. A none-too-hardy evergreen shrub from South Africa, it gives of its best, I find, if cut to the ground each spring. If you do not do this and if its old shoots survive the winter, they will flower the following year, but this is not usually a notable event, the flowers murky chocolate in colour but, worse, the shrub becomes leggy and scrawny. Far better, then, to make it start again. We don't cut it down till early spring (which is the normal practice with slightly tender shrubs) and in the winter its old stems provide anchorage for wads of protective fern fronds which we stuff between them.

Melianthus major takes time to get going in the following season and is, ironically, at its peak in early December, just before

▲ *The solid structure of newly clipped* Osmanthus delavayi *is softened by a self-sown* Olearia solandri. *This great favourite with us wafts the fragrance of heliotrope through the Barn Garden at all times of the year. The dwarf lilac,* Syringa meyeri *var.* spontanea *'Palibin', is a filler with a short but welcome season.*

▼ Phlomis fruticosa *is a wide-spreading anchor plant near the border's margin. Here, in early August, it has lately been dead-headed after a prolonged flowering season. Rosa 'The Fairy' can be seen to the right, masquerading as a phlox. Border phloxes love our heavy soil. In rather surprising contrast is the giant poker,* Kniphofia uvaria *'Nobilis'.*

a sharp frost smites it. But it is good all through the autumn. Large, pinnate leaves (they smell of peanut butter, if bruised), smooth and glaucous, each leaflet incurved and revealing its marginal toothing, which is very pronounced. It looks its best in low sunlight, when shadows are cast by one toothy leaflet margin on to another's flatter surface. An extraordinary feeling of depth is created. Do you believe me? I hope so, but if you come from the North Island of New Zealand, where *M. major* was introduced and has run riot, being described as a noxious weed, you will hate it automatically. We judge plants, as also people, by association and by the way they behave to and with us.

Many of our best foliage shrubs are on the borderlines of hardiness, the irony being that if they weren't they might easily become pestilential. New Zealand flax, *Phormium tenax*, is one such. It is generally classified as a shrub, but you could argue that point. It throws up wadges of sword leaves from ground level, perhaps to 2.5m/8ft or more, if well pleased and is often used as a windbreak near the sea. Although it is naturally green, the deep purple *P. t.* Purpureum Group is normally used. Left to its own devices, it forms colonies that become thick and shapeless.

But it is of *Phormium cookianum* that I want to write. This is a less vigorous, shorter species and its leaves are flexible and arching. We greatly value the clone *P. c.* subsp. *hookeri* 'Tricolor', in which the leaves are striped green, pinkish purple (on the leaf margins) and cream, with intermediate shades where two colours overlap. Seen close to or at a distance, it is a splendid plant, but, as so often, it looks best if kept to a small crown. As it hates being moved and sulks for a year afterwards, we simply chop pieces off ours to reduce its size. An additional asset is its flowering, in May, followed by pleasing seed pods. The plant is normally 1.2m/4ft or so high, but flowering doubles this. It contrasts well with dark colours, as of yew or osmanthus, but also with something like a not-too-vigorous cardoon, *Cynara cardunculus*, with jagged, grey-green leaves. And it never has an off-season.

The hybrid between *Fatsia japonica* and an ivy, × *Fatshedera lizei* is a brilliant anchor plant for deep but moist shade. I have it in the sunless angle of a wall and the house and, with its glossy, light-reflecting leaves, which are quite large and important-looking, it compellingly focuses your attention. × *Fatshedera*, having a climber as one parent, is by nature a lolling plant that leans on its elbow, and this is the way you normally see it. But I have pruned mine so that it remains upright to 2m/6ft. Behind

▲ Cistus × purpureus *is one of the earliest of this gummy tribe, whose aromatic fragrance so often fills the air. It is light magenta and here, probably accidentally, combines with a fairly dwarf form of the cardoon,* Cynara cardunculus, *which was given to me from the Chelsea Physic Garden. It is more than usually cut-leaved and covered with prickles.*

▼ *Even the darkest corners of your garden will be given life by the glossy, light-reflecting* × Fatshedera lizei. *It is in marked contrast to the solemn, heavy-leaved* Clerodendrum bungei *behind it. This suckering sub-shrub itself is jollified by domes of deep pink, scented blossom from August onwards, but it does need a protected position to bring its old wood through the winter.*

▼ The rusty brown hummock is where the dormant buds of the soft shield fern, Polystichum setiferum 'Pulcherrimum Bevis', lie huddled together, waiting to unfurl new fronds in front of Spiraea japonica 'Goldflame'. Now, in March and into April, the spiraea is flushed with young, copper-coloured shoots, and there's a display of hyacinths beneath it.

▶ The same scene ten weeks later. The bulbs are dormant beneath Spiraea japonica 'Goldflame', now with its mature yellowy-green foliage and flowering with deep pink corymbs. The twice-divided (bipinnate) fronds of Polystichum setiferum 'Pulcherrimum Bevis' have unfurled to rub cheeks with the spiraea and they will be the main attraction after we have given the shrub its annual pruning. We remove the fern's old fronds in spring, when light is required by the sprouting hyacinths.

it and in complete contrast is the exceptionally dark *Clerodendrum bungei*, with big, heart-shaped leaves. That is a deciduous sub-shrub and is underplanted with snowdrops and self-sowing Welsh poppies, *Meconopsis cambrica*. Then comes a path and, on the other side of that, *Fatsia japonica* itself, a big old specimen, but it responds well to pruning and I remove enough of its lowest branches to make space for the light airiness of a 1m/3ft fern of great style, *Polystichum setiferum* 'Pulcherrimum Bevis', whose fronds are drawn into a tail at the tips. Beside and in front of that are lower-growing ferns, *P. s.* Plumosodivisilobum Group. With both these the fronds can remain in position for a whole year, staying green, but if you cut them back in January to make room for snowdrops, they won't object.

VALUABLE DECIDUOUS SHRUBS

Shrubs may be deciduous and no less valuable as anchor plants. *Cotoneaster horizontalis* is an incredibly versatile species with a fishbone structure, good when in leaf, which it is from February to December, as also in the brief season when it is bare. Planted against a wall, of any aspect, it accepts the challenge and climbs without assistance. Planted on the flat, as it might be on the top and edge of a retaining wall, it forms a stiff horizontal bracket. It flowers in spring, with insects crowding to its otherwise incon-spicuous display. The crimson berries ripen in fall and, if not devoured by birds, are joined in November by the magenta colour-ing of its dying foliage. The party ends only in December and there is not a long to wait till February.

You want to be on the lookout for shrubs with several seasons of interest, perhaps even year-round. Consider the whole range of assets – leaves and stems, flowers, berries, seed heads. Don't choose a dull plant like a tree peony. Glamorous though it is in flower, it has nothing else on offer.

Spiraea japonica 'Goldflame' is not a beautiful shrub in itself but it does beautiful things. When it flushes with young shoots in spring, they are copper-coloured and one wants to make use of this asset. I have underplanted with hyacinths – pink, blue and pale yellow. These flower in March. The recommended technique for pruning the spiraea is to cut all its branches back by half in March. But if I did that, its new coppery growth would not get going until after the hyacinths had finished flowering. The shrub flowers with deep pink corymbs at the turn of June–July, which is its second high-point, and I find that if I prune it as soon as the

flower heads turn brown, the small amount of young growth that it makes before all growth ceases for the winter will start up again in March, so as exactly to coincide with the hyacinths. This kind of manipulation is endlessly fascinating and you have to find it out for yourself.

A plant must be judged not merely for itself but on how you have used it and what it adds up to in its setting. Spiraeas can be dull, philadelphus and deutzias too. Yet *Philadelphus coronarius* 'Aureus' is a winner if treated correctly, by pruning out its old wood immediately after flowering. Plant it in part shade, say against a north wall, to prevent scorch. Watering in times of drought will also help it. Such are the requirements of many golden-leaved plants: hostas, for instance, and the elder, *Sambucus racemosa* 'Plumosa Aurea'.

With manipulation the dogwood, *Cornus alba* 'Elegantissima', is one of the most valued plants in my garden and is a key player in a succession planting, with *Bupleurum fruticosum* playing a supporting role. Another mixed-border shrub that acts both as protagonist and as foil is *Viburnum opulus* 'Compactum', a slightly dwarfened selection of our native guelder rose. I wrote about it

earlier (page 25). Pruning needs to be intelligent, so that parts of the shrub will flower and fruit this year, while other parts will make non-flowering growth that will perform in the following year. If it flowers and fruits all over, it will make no young shoots on which to perform in the following year. It will get into a state of biennial bearing, as we say of fruit trees. If an 'on' year is coming up, prune out at least two thirds of those promising young shoots that would otherwise contribute to exhausting the shrub with flower and berry the next year. Where you have cut, it will then make young shoots (instead of flowers) the following year and these will flower and fruit the year after. In this way you achieve a balance.

A good flowering shrub must have something extra. Variegated leaves may be an asset, contributing lightness of touch. Most weigelas are desperately dull in heavy green leaf. *Weigela* 'Florida Variegata' is the oldest shrub in my Long Border, yet seems, helped by pruning, to retain eternal youth. It carries an abundance of pink, scented flowers in spring, but doesn't look middle-aged after that. Its cream-edged leaves go on contributing until late autumn, when the margins take on rosy tints before December leaf-fall.

▲ **Summer foliage colour** *in another year, with vivid* Solenostemon *hybrids, grown from seed.*

▼ **Mid December**: *the dogwood's leaves have fallen, revealing its young carmine stems which look especially good in winter sunshine. Wallflowers are bedded out in front to provide an April–May show.*

▶▼ **Early March**: *underneath the dogwood we grow a late-flowering snowdrop (Galanthus plicatus 'Washfield Warham'). Other small, early-spring-flowering bulbs, like blue × Chionoscilla allenii and the small, yellow trumpet daffodil, Narcissus minor, come through later to flower around the same space.*

Himalayacalamus falconeri *is an elegant bamboo if pruned in a certain way.*

▼ **In early March** *we cut out every cane that is more than one season old.*

▲ *For several weeks, with the only culms remaining being the young, unbranched ones of the*

previous summer's growth, the bamboo gleams olive green – it is unmissable.

▶ **In May–June**, *the bamboo's appearance changes dramatically when it becomes all feathery and flexible with young foliage; this is easily bowed down by rainfall, but straightens afterwards. A self-sown* Aruncus dioicus *in front.*

GRASSES AND BAMBOOS

Ornamental grasses are a huge subject and have been much in vogue for some time now. They are best used as a contrast to broader leaves. Their length of season often depends on their exposure to the elements. One of the most dependable for three quarters of the year is *Calamagrostis* × *acutiflora* 'Karl Foerster'. When, at 2m/6ft, it flowers in late June, it is purple and all soft fluffiness. Rain will sway it to the ground, but it usually recovers itself on drying out. At the end of flowering, its stems stiffen and remain bolt upright till we cut them back the following March. They also bleach and become a landscape feature, with an air of importance even at a distance. It is a winner.

Miscanthus, as a genus, is so widely grown that a trial was held for it in a rather out-of-the-way part of the RHS garden at Wisley. I grow quite a few of them, including *M. sinensis* 'Silberfeder', already mentioned. A favourite with us is *M. sinensis* 'Strictus'. It is a zebra grass, which is to say that its green leaves are cross-banded with yellow. Similar, and perhaps better known is *M. s.* 'Zebrinus', but that has quite a floppy habit, whereas 'Strictus' remains boldly upright to 2.25m/7ft or so and is a great mixer, I find, above a range of hydrangeas and other contrasting shrubs. Grasses excel in contrast. They should seldom be herded together.

I am even more enamoured of specimen-forming bamboos, the big grass relations. If you look after them, by regularly thinning out and removing the old culms (canes), they never accumulate a whole lot of dead leaves and you get a feeling of light airiness because you can see through and past a colony. Some bamboos look jaded in winter, but most of the *Phyllostachys* remain fresh and invigorating.

Himalayacalamus falconeri (syn. *Arundinaria falconeri*) is a remarkable bamboo if its pruning is treated in a certain way. In summer it is a graceful mass of foliage, with flexible stems that are apt to be weighted to the ground when wet. It needs siting where this won't matter. It is not cast-iron hardy and is thus not pruned till early March. At that time we remove all second-year (or older) culms, which announce their age by their fluffiness and holding on to some of last year's foliage. What remains are the youngest culms, easily identified because they are upright, unbranched rods, virtually leafless. They are smooth, shiny and olive green. The colony will by now consist of nothing but these and they are amazing to contemplate. Presently, of course, they themselves leaf out and the cycle is repeated.

▲ Asplenium scolopen-drium, *the hartstongue fern, is found in lime-rich soils from the Isle of Wight to northwest Scotland. Of its own accord it discovered our only original garden wall, which was cemented with limy mortar, and has colonized at the base and in the mortar itself. Being evergreen, it remains a handsome feature, but it is wise to cut away old fronds towards the end of March, before this operation damages the newly emerging crop.*

▼ *By those who see only bright colours* Paris poly-phylla *is often overlooked or deliberately ignored, but it has a beautiful structure that those of us who do not require a permanent diet of garish colours greatly appreciate. It has a very long season of beauty, from late May to October, and combines well with the featheriness of ferns, here the lady fern,* Athyrium filix-femina *'Plumosum Axminster'. Both plants enjoy moist, heavy soil in part shade.*

FERNS FOR DIFFERENT SEASONS

Ferns, which I mentioned tangentially at the beginning of this chapter, are a great asset in many ways, each of them coming fully into its own at different seasons. For instance, the plain-leaved hartstongue fern, *Asplenium scolopendrium*, which likes lime and has sown itself all along the bottom of a wall that sheds limy old mortar, is fully revealed in winter, when the plants occupying the border in front of it have died or been cut down. *Polypodium inter-jectum* 'Cornubiense' does not acquire its new fronds till July, but they are fresh and bright green through the winter and an admir-able foil to the sombre darkness of my hermaphrodite butcher's broom, *Ruscus aculeatus*, which, however, is covered thickly with red berries from autumn through to the following summer.

Dryopteris wallichiana is possibly at its most arresting in May as its bright green young fronds, thickly coated with brown scales, unfurl with snaky suggestiveness. It makes perfect individual funnels, 1m/3ft high, and they last till the following spring. But the little maidenhair fern, *Adiantum venustum*, makes a carpet and ground cover around shrubs, as it might be hydrangeas, and it never needs attention. The old fronds disappear discreetly in due course, being overtaken by young ones as early as March.

STRUCTURAL PERENNIALS

Some perennial plants contribute to the structural element in a garden. It may be on a large scale like *Gunnera manicata*, which comes into the next chapter, or it may be small like the wild ginger, *Asarum europaeum*, whose light-reflecting leaves I described on page 32.

Many perennials are grown mainly for their foliage. *Paris polyphylla*, for instance. At 1m/3ft or so, above naked scapes, it makes a ring of horizontally held leaves, ten or eleven of them, while in the centre is the flower, again of muted colouring, but its seed pods ripen and split open to reveal brilliant orange or red berries. So it has a double season and keeps you guessing. It likes shade, so we sometimes underplant it with shade-loving bedding-out plants, like begonias, which give you a tremendous range of choice. It also blends well with ferns.

Hostas are an obvious shade-tolerant choice. If you have no luck in keeping slugs and snails at bay, grow rodgersias instead. Their leaves are tough and pests do not attack them. I can recommend one or other variety of *Rodgersia pinnata*, and 'Maurice Mason' in particular for its foliage and flowers over a long season (see

pages 22–3). *Rodgersia podophylla* is seen at its best in the cool, moist climate of northwest Scotland. Podophylla means foot-shaped, referring to the leaflets, set about an arc, which resemble webbed ducks' feet. A handsome deciduous perennial, it is of little value in my garden where, even in a shaded position, summer heat scorches it disastrously. In western Scotland, however, it sails through and the foliage changes in autumn to bright shades of pink. Excellent by the side of a pool, where its reflection gives double value.

We may not be well informed about the turbulent history of the Chatham Islands, which lie in the Pacific to the east of New Zealand, but they are the home of the Chatham Island forget-me-not (*Myosotidium hortensia*), of which gardeners are so proud in the west Scottish climate, and of *Astelia chathamica*, which is a good structural perennial. It is none too hardy but we have been lucky with it through a number of successive winters. Being evergreen, it needs to see the light, but, when low temperatures are forecast, we give it a plastic *surtout* stuffed with fern fronds. It makes slowly increasing clumps, rather like phormiums. The leaves are grey-green, spear-like but flexible, so as to reveal different sides of the same leaf, the underside notably paler and more silvery than the upper. It is a plant that shows up from a great distance and year-round. My best-placed specimen is at the top of the Long Border, not in the border itself but on the other side of the adjacent path. It is at one end of the Lutyens-designed seat, with which the view terminates.

Acanthus are always with us and, being evergreen, are often cited as herbaceous alternatives to shrubs (why you should need an alternative to shrubs is unclear). Their leaves can be uncomfortably spiny. Not so *Acanthus mollis* (it does get mildew) and my pick here is *A. mollis* 'Hollard's Gold'. Its lime-green foliage is at its brightest in late winter and early spring. After that it gets a bit dull, but you should plant it far enough back from your viewing point for other plants to be able to grow up in front of it. The acanthus will then have a subsidiary season when it flowers, the spikes rising above its foreground (if you have chosen your foreground so as to enable this to happen). *A. spinosus* is seen best as a landscape plant in big groups. It is a toughie.

A border consisting entirely of structural trees, shrubs and perennials would quickly bore, but don't let that tempt you into omitting anchor plants altogether. They are a core necessity in the overall scheme, the foundation on which to build a succession of interest.

▲ The young growth of Rodgersia podophylla *is attractively flushed. In cool climates this flush is retained right through the summer. The foliage tends to brown badly in the southeast where I come from and is quite unsightly from midsummer on. This rodgersia likes cool, moist conditions and some shade, which we certainly give it, but it's just not enough.*

▼ Astelia chathamica *is a bold anchor plant on the verge of hardiness, but if it comes through the winter it makes a wonderful focal point, even from a great distance. The leaves twist to reveal the pale undersides, so it seems to have more life than you expect in a plant. At the top end of the Long Border, it shows up well against the dark yew hedge.*

Acer palmatum 'Shishigashira'

Japanese maple
Height: 4m/12ft
Spread: 2m/6ft
Hardy, sun or partial shade
Compact, upright, with crimped, jagged, dark green leaves that colour up in late autumn, this tree performs in every season. Young leaf buds are red, the web of young shoots behind them overlaid by a soft grey bloom.

▶ Aucuba japonica

Height and spread: up to 3m/10ft
Hardy, prefers shade
My plant is male and a well-spotted form. It acts as a pollinator for *A. japonica* f. *longifolia*, which is female and fruits freely. Both perform reliable anchoring jobs in my Long Border. I am fond of my heavily yellow-spotted laurel (although this kind of undisciplined variegation is widely detested), but have to admit that in early summer quite a high proportion of its leaves scorch to brown in patches. This happened less before the shade from a nearby mulberry disappeared following the big storm of October 1987. But my bush is healthy, by and large, and I am prepared to pick off its worst leaves by hand.

▲ Catalpa bignonioides 'Aurea'

Indian bean tree
Height and spread: up to 4.5m/15ft annually
Hardy, sun
Cut back each winter to a 1.5m/5ft framework, the golden catalpa makes a splendid foliage plant, with big (25cm/10in) leaves at or just above eye level, bronze when young but freshest yellow up to leaf-fall. Plants have to be grafted and this is done in Holland, which makes them expensive.

Cornus alba 'Elegantissima'

Dogwood
Height and spread: 1.5m/5ft (pruned)
Hardy, sun
This makes a thoroughly dull shrub unless it is pruned every year. We cut ours back to 60cm–1m/ 2–3ft in March, take out a third of the oldest shoots and manure generously. Then the plant has a dual role – carmine stems in winter and green leaves with a broad, white margin in summer that are a good backdrop to any sort of bedding-out of any colour.

◀ Cotoneaster horizontalis

Herringbone cotoneaster
Height and spread: 3m/10ft against a wall, undulating horizontally in the open
Hardy, sun or shade
This incredibly versatile shrub has a stiff, fishbone structure, yet is full of curves. It is good in leaf from February to December. Bare and rimed with frost, it is irresistible to photographers. New foliage is already expanding in February. Inconspicuous flowers lead to crimson berries in fall, set among crimson foliage. I have to be ruthless with misplaced seedlings, spread around the garden thanks to the birds' liking for the berries.

▲ × Fatshedera lizei

Tree ivy
Height: 3m/10ft
Spread: up to 2m/6ft
Hardy, shade
This is a decumbent (lolling), non-climbing, evergreen shrub with rusty young growth that becomes lustrous green. The largish, ivy-like leaves are 10–24cm/4–10in long. I prune mine so that it remains upright to 2m/6ft.

▲ **Osmanthus delavayi**
Height and spread:
2–2.5m/6–8ft
Hardy, sun
This can be a large and shapeless bush, without the gardener's manipulating hand. Thousands of little, tubular, white flowers appear at the turn of March–April on the previous year's shoots, their scent lasting longer than the pristine whiteness of the flowers, which start turning brown after a week or so. We clip our bushes to retain their bulbous shapes as soon as the display is past.

▶ **Paulownia tomentosa**
Foxglove tree
Height: 4.2m/14ft annually
Spread: 2m/6ft
Hardy, sun
This normally grows to 12m/40ft, has rounded, furry leaves of no great shakes and bears clusters of foxglove-like flowers in spring, unless you do as I do. First, over two or three years, establish a young plant from seed or root cuttings. Cut it almost to the ground each winter, allowing only one or two shoots to develop next spring. These will make up to 4.2m/14ft in one season and will bear only a few rough-textured leaves, each upwards of 1m/3ft across.

Philadelphus coronarius 'Aureus'
Golden-leaved mock orange
Height: 4m/12ft
Spread: 4m/12ft
Hardy, partial shade
Like many golden-leaved plants, this is liable to scorch in full sun, but not if you treat it as a foliage plant and prune out its flowered growth immediately after its May flowering. Its leaves are ravishingly fresh in spring and its young growth remains attractive over a long season.

▼ **Phlomis fruticosa**
Jerusalem sage
Height: 1.2m/4ft
Spread: 4m/12ft
Hardy, sun
A sprawling shrub with grey-green leaves. It carries whorls of yellow, labiate flowers over a long season in June–July. We remove these when they are beginning to look tired, just as bright pink and mauve phloxes start flowering nearby.

◀ **Phormium cookianum subsp. hookeri 'Tricolor'**
New Zealand flax
Height: 1.2m/4ft (double in flower)
Spread: 5m/15ft
Hardy, sun
Flexible, arching leaves are striped green, pinkish purple (on the leaf margins) and cream, with intermediate shades where two colours overlap. We keep ours to a small crown by chopping pieces off. Its tubular, yellow-green flowers, in May, are followed by pleasing seed pods.

▼ **Prunus laurocerasus 'Otto Luyken'**
Cherry laurel
Height: 2m/6ft (pruned)
Spread: 3m/10ft (pruned)
Hardy, sun or shade
I keep this evergreen laurel, with glossy, light-reflecting foliage, to a height of less than 2m/6ft. Although principally a foliage plant, it has white and fragrant flowers in clustered spikelets in spring and again in late summer, after which we cut it back by removing the flowered shoots.

▼ **Weigela 'Florida Variegata'**
Height: 2.25m/7ft
Spread: 2.5m/8ft
Hardy, sun
A compact weigela with variegated foliage is an asset and this one is bowed down with swags of pale pink funnels, sweetly scented, in May. The foliage remains an asset into December, shedding very late. We prune out the flowering shoots in winter to encourage new flowering stems and to keep the shrub in shape.

PERENNIALS & BULBS

that share the same space

With our sights always focused on getting best value over a long season – the ethic of 'I'm not greedy but I like a lot' – we constantly plan so that when a plant has its off-season another takes over.

The idea of plants sharing the same space is that they do this without getting in each other's way. You want to think of one plant providing the main display and to concentrate your main focus on that, but then to find an off-season partner that will bridge the gap without doing any harm to the principal.

Each plant is an individual case and will need individual treatment. Some are tough enough to withstand any number of partners sharing their bed space, but others do not like competition at all and will suffer from it. And each site is different, too, although the same plants may flourish in varying circumstances.

Spring-flowering woodlanders and bulbs are often ideal off-season subjects for our purpose. Bulbs that flower in spring do so before deciduous shrubs and before many mainstay perennials have rubbed the sleep out of their eyes and become active. You need to consider the habit and vigour of both the protagonist and its partner(s). *Hemerocallis* 'Marion Vaughn' is a strong perennial that can cope with narcissi, having broader than usual but still narrow leaves. I like to use one or other of the Triandrus or Cyclamineus types, like *Narcissus* 'Dove Wings'. As their lanky leaves die off, those of the daylily, lanky in the same way, take over and it flowers for a long summer season. What you must never use in any part of a mixed border are broad-leaved daffodils, but I constantly see this mistake being made. They are far too aggressive, overlaying

◀ *The majority of crocosmias are invaluable for flowering rather later than most other bulbs or corms.* Crocosmia × crocosmiiflora *'Star of the East' has a long August season and its apricot-orange colouring contrasts ideally with late-flowering* Agapanthus *'Loch Hope'. Unfortunately, agapanthus do not relish the company of other plants and are usually grown on their own for that reason. We grow them in pots until they have made their flower buds and we are confident of securing our catch. We then introduce them to gaps left for the purpose. The May–June-flowering* Allium hollandicum *'Purple Sensation' prolongs the season, its globes retaining their shape for weeks.*

57

This succession, comprising Narcissus 'Dove Wings', Hemerocallis 'Marion Vaughn' (the main protagonist) and Phlox paniculata, spans a period of five months.

▼ **At the beginning of March** *the foliage of Narcissus 'Dove Wings' is similar in appearance to the slightly paler green straps of emerging Hemerocallis 'Marion Vaughn'.*

▼ ▼ **By the end of March** *the junior partner, Narcissus 'Dove Wings', is in flower, white with a cream cup. This is a Cyclamineus type of daffodil, the flowers having a prominent corona and segments that are recurved. More important in a mixed border planting is the foliage, which is narrow and lightweight enough to be concealed by developing daylily foliage as the narcissus die off. The day lilies are interplanted with Phlox paniculata.*

neighbours, and look a mess for many weeks after flowering. If you tie their foliage into knots they look even worse.

Once bulbs disappear, you may be afraid of chawing into them with a spade while they are dormant. The answer to that problem is that they will be protected from damage by the proximity of the plants around which you have sited them. Suppose you planted winter aconites (*Eranthis hyemalis*) around your hostas, which works really well. The hostas' leaves will form an umbrella around the aconites snoozing underneath, just where you wouldn't dream of getting busy with a digging tool.

In some cases, you need to mark the position of bulbs (I use short pieces of weathered bamboo cane). We plant the little red-

▼ **Mid July** *and Hemero-callis 'Marion Vaughn' is flowering with mauve* Phlox paniculata, *a strain given to me by Margery Fish from its native USA. Like most of the yellow daylilies, the colour which is most natural to hemerocallis, this one is sweetly scented. We do have to watch for tiny maggots inside the flower buds, which inflate them unnaturally, and control the problem by spraying.*

flowered species tulip, *T. linifolia*, which has very narrow leaves, among *Glaucium flavum* f. *fulvum* at the front of the Long Border and we do not want to disturb the tulips when replanting the poppies. Each bloom of this coppery-orange form of our native horned poppy, so called because of its long, thin seed pods, curved like horns, lasts for just one day, but its leaves are even more significant than its flowers. They form a basal rosette and are felted grey, with sinuous margins. This is generally biennial and needs frequent replacing, but we are ready for that, growing a fresh batch of seedlings every year. With most of the display so close to the ground, any interplanted bulb needs to be small and *Tulipa linifolia*, which can be left from year to year, does the job admirably.

Japanese anemones are protagonists that offer opportunities for succession plantings before they flower in late summer. Our favourite is the single white Anemone × hybrida 'Honorine Jobert'. It is slow off the mark and a sequence of bulbs in the same space gives earlier interest.

▲ **In earliest spring** *the green-leaved snowdrop, Galanthus × allenii, is flowering, followed in late March by hyacinths, whose scent is wafted on the air. (There is an oak bench right by this area, if it is dry enough to sit on.) The foliage of tulips and alliums is already visible.*

▲ **By the third week in April** *the Darwinhybrid tulip 'Apeldoorn' is out, already surrounded by the foliage of Allium cristophii and emerging anemone leaves.*

▲ **In May and June** *the mauve globes of Allium cristophii on 60cm/2ft stems join the party in a sea of anemone foliage. The allium leaves die off discreetly, hidden by the anemones.*

▶ **By August** *the anemone is into its stride; it has a very long flowering season that starts in July. The allium flowers retain their shape for many weeks after the colour has faded.*

▶ **Early September** *and the anemone is 1.2m/4ft tall. Given moisture and part shade, it will continue flowering into October.*

Snowdrops have many demands placed on them when they have the garden largely to themselves at their time of flowering. They alternate admirably with deciduous ferns. I also have them among my *Polystichum setiferum* cultivars. These, the soft shield ferns, retain their old fronds in a fresh condition right through the winter, but have no objection to being cut back a bit early, where I have interplanted them with snowdrops. So that would be in early January, as soon as I see the snowdrops showing through. I mustn't delay this cutting back through inattention, otherwise the snowdrops, kept in the dark, will get drawn.

I have common snowdrops running through my phloxes (*Phlox paniculata*) in the Long Border. Some of the phloxes are among the branches of my old *Phlomis fruticosa*, already described, which gives the snowdrops the chance to clump up and self-sow. In other areas of phlox, they may have to be disturbed from time to time. A point to make is that you don't want to have a large and somewhat aggressive snowdrop near the phloxes, as the latter's young shoots, already growing in February, can be weakened and the phloxes are our main protagonists.

I also grow snowdrops under my *Fuchsia* 'Genii', the one with lime-green foliage. If that retains live stems throughout the winter, I simply cut them back by half to 45cm/18in or less when the snowdrops need to be seen. By the side of fuchsia and snowdrops, a thick group of self-sowing *Tulipa sprengeri*, last of all the tulips in flower, is at its peak usually in late May.

Under the northeast side of our house, I combine *Gentiana asclepiadea* with snowdrops, as well as with the freely self-seeding *Scilla bithynica*, *Cyclamen hederifolium* and, over all, deciduous male ferns, *Dryopteris filix-mas*. The willow gentian is a European wilding of woodland, so it is good for August flowering in any shady part of your garden.

Galanthus 'Atkinsii' is a sterile, January-flowering snowdrop of considerable vigour, its bulbs quickly multiplying into big clumps. It is planted over and among dormant perennials in a damp, northwest-facing bed, notably rodgersias, *Euphorbia palustris*, hostas, *Carex elata* 'Aurea' (Bowles's golden) and *Aralia cachemirica*. The snowdrop leaves, before dying off, lie around so thickly that they give me qualms lest the perennials should be unable to penetrate this carpet. But they always manage in the end. When the perennials need dividing, we have to lift the snowdrops, but we return most of them and spread the rest elsewhere in the garden.

◄ The climax of this sequence of plantings is the Fuchsia 'Genii', which has lime-green foliage and flowers in September (bottom). This is why the teazel that has sown itself into it has already turned autumnal. While the fuchsia is developing, it allows space first for snow-

drops in March (top), and in late May (middle) for the latest-flowering of all tulip species, Tulipa sprengeri. This sets seed abundantly, which is why it has made a dense colony.

▲ In early February the foliage of hardy Cyclamen hederifolium (top left),

which is in condition from early autumn right through to the following May (when it dies off), is joined by the common snowdrop, Galanthus nivalis. We have cut down the male fern, Dryopteris filix-mas, to leave rust-coloured crowns that will unfurl new fronds in early summer.

In March self-sown Scilla bithynica (top right) makes a pale blue carpet beneath a cotoneaster on the north-facing corner of our larder. It is a good filler among common male, Dryopteris filix-mas, or other deciduous ferns and is grown far less than its obliging nature deserves.

Mid August, in the same shady area as the scilla, we can now see the male fern in full fig (above) and, enjoying similar conditions at the front, Gentiana asclepiadea, the willow gentian. The lawn does not contain grass of the best quality!

▲ *Showiest of the* Anemone blanda *cultivars is the dazzling 'White Splendour', equally at home in sun or shade. Here it is seen in April in brilliant sunshine at the foot of a wall shrub,* Cestrum parqui, *which is still dormant. The shrub's moribund wood has been removed to make way for branches that have come through the winter and are breaking into new growth.*

▼ *Now the anemone has gone to ground and the space it occupies has been engulfed by* Cestrum parqui *which flowers on old wood for four months from late June. The flowers are half closed by day but expand in the evening and are delicately scented. However, the scent is not switched on until ten in the evening, so we cut a spray to enjoy indoors.*

SPRING WOODLANDERS

Summer-dormant plants can share space with summer-flowering plants, the latter being the principals and our focus being summer. All deciduous woodland perennials that flower in spring and up to the end of May, when the overhead leaf canopy becomes really heavy, are summer-dormant and allow you a great range of choice. These woodland plants are different in different parts of the world, but any of them would be appropriate to our purpose as fillers in the off-season.

One of my favourite hostas is the grey- or should I say glaucous-leaved 'Krossa Regal'. It has a proud and stylish, notably upright habit of growth. Coming quite late into leaf, in May, it is surrounded with the bright yellow little European windflower, *Anemone ranunculoides*. Both plants like some shade. It is a shame that the anemone doesn't grow wild in Britain. I fancy the English Channel must have cut off its progress northwards just too soon. This anemone, like many of its kind, has a creeping habit and grows right over the top of the hosta's crown, but is pushed aside, as it is going over, by the hosta's strong shoots.

Of all the spring-flowering anemones, blue-flowered forms of *Anemone blanda* are probably the most popular. I remember this species flowering, in April, beneath a canopy of wild cedars of Lebanon, in Lebanon, but the bluish colouring was weak. Clearly

▲ Geranium × riversleaianum 'Mavis Simpson' is one of several long-flowering cranesbills whose growth starts from a restricted base but increases in range over a period of many months. Early in the season there is plenty of space around it, here occupied by the early-spring-flowering bulbous Iris reticulata.

▲ ▶ Geranium albanum makes a ground-hugging mat and has mauve-pink flowers in April–May, at the same time as self-sown forget-me-nots. After flowering it disappears completely until the autumn, its space being permanently occupied by a late starter, the ginger lily, Hedychium densiflorum, which flowers in August and September with dense spikes of biscuit-coloured flowers. G. albanum is mixed up here with 'Dilys', a cranesbill of a similar low and spreading habit, which flowers from May to November. Behind is the spring-flowering Weigela 'Praecox Variegata' whose lower branches, heavy with tubular blossom, have joined the ground party.

you have to seek out or breed the bluest you can find. It is then a lot bluer than you ever see *A. apennina*. There are many selected variants, including the shocking-pink *A. blanda* 'Radar', which I can't help loving, though it is not easy to use.

For my money, *Anemone blanda* 'White Splendour' is well named. It seems to be the strongest-growing of the lot, with the largest flowers of its kind, opening in the right weather to blinding-white discs. And it is versatile. We have it in two quite different situations. The first is in partial shade beneath deciduous hortensia hydrangeas, whose young foliage is still only half expanded, though these are obviously the principals when their turn comes, late June onwards. But 'White Splendour' gets along famously beneath them.

The other site is just about the sunniest one could find, in front of the deciduous, green-flowered *Cestrum parqui*, which is loosely trained against a sunny wall. We prune that back towards the wall when we can see how much of its wood has come through the winter and is breaking into new growth, and how much is moribund or dead and can be pruned away. At this stage there is a lot of bare ground in front of the cestrum that will later be entirely overshadowed by its summer growth. What better for that spring space than *Anemone blanda* 'White Splendour'?

And there are other spring performers around here, so it doesn't feel lonely. Various hybrids of *Iris reticulata*, for instance.

▼ Geranium *'Ann Folkard'* flowers from late May to the end of October, its circumference increasing throughout this period. The space around it earlier is occupied by bulbs, notably camassias, and by vigorous bulbous irises. Here, in the July section of its run, its vivid magenta-purple flowers, with a compelling dark eye, are framed by Euphorbia schillingii, Hydrangea arborescens 'Annabelle', Delphinium 'Mighty Atom' and pure white Ammi majus.

These hybrids may be showier than the species itself, but I am very fond of the species straight and am grateful that it flowers in February, even before you'd given it a thought. By itself it is a fairly sombre colour, so I have interplanted it with a modest yet strong-growing snowdrop (given to me by Margery Fish), *Galanthus nivalis* 'Tiny'.

BULBS WITH RAMBLING CRANESBILLS

These irises and snowdrops are in the space later to be occupied by a rambling cranesbill that increases its ground covering through its season, the pink *Geranium × riversleaianum* 'Mavis Simpson'. Brian Halliwell, when he was still working at Kew, gave me that. 'Who is Mavis Simpson?' I enquired. 'She's there,' said Brian, nodding towards a gardener, working in his domain. In its season, *G. r.* 'Mavis Simpson' is protecting the now dormant bulbs of iris and snowdrop. Itself is quite a short-lived perennial, I should mention, so you need to propagate it frequently from basal cuttings taken in its winter resting season.

Geranium 'Ann Folkard' is a prime example of a butch geranium that goes out into the world to explore. In spring it gets going very slowly from a basal crown of leaves. But you need to leave a lot of space around it in the knowledge that that will be filled in due course. So you can plant quite strong bulbs – Dutch and English bulbous irises, camassias, perhaps ixias. As these go dormant, 'Ann Folkard' takes full command. It starts flowering in the last days of May and, because it keeps on making new growth, flowering continues into autumn, the plant occupying more and more space. It is better not to let it ramble at will, or that space will be altogether excessive. We make it a cage of brushwood so that it is more or less contained and can rise to 1.2m/4ft or so. Meantime, of course, the bulbs have long since gone to rest, but will reappear once more when their turn comes round.

Geranium wallichianum has an equally long season, but starts exploring from the start. It can penetrate and overlay many neighbours with a light flowering mantle and in such a way that it becomes hard to tell from exactly where it originally started.

TACTFUL INFILLING

A clump-forming geranium like *G. himalayense*, that keeps more or less in the same place but flowers for quite a limited season, needs different treatment. I grow this under a bush of the hybrid musk rose 'Felicia'. After flowering, in early June, the geranium is cut right back all over. It quickly makes new leaves and these serve as a background to the rose's pink flowers. 'Felicia', if dead-headed, itself will carry a second flush.

As I have said, some plants would like to be loners. *Aster sedifolius* (syn. *A. acris*) is a good example of one that resents competition. At 1m/3ft, it has a tightly packed quilt of little, mauve, lop-sided daisies in August–September. In the winter it dies back

▲ Aster sedifolius, *seen here in April through* Libertia peregrinans *and behind* Spiraea japonica *'Gold Mound', makes low cushions of green in winter and early spring. These must not be shaded out, so we plant tulips thinly among them but more densely behind and in front.*

▼ Aster sedifolius, *generously supported by peasticks, flowers at 1.2m/4ft in August and can now bear the competition from self-sowing nasturtiums forming a thin mantle on top.*

to a ground-level cushion of green shoots which see it through that season, but they must not be darkened by neighbours. That said, a little tactful infilling may be practised harmlessly. Say you were planting one variety of tulip both behind and in front of your groups of *Aster sedifolius*. The latter will be spaced some 35cm/14in apart. You could sparsely pop in a very few bulbs of the same tulip halfway across this gap, which would make a link, yet without overlaying the asters. Don't choose a broad-leaved, smothering tulip. It will flower, and as it finishes flowering the aster can gradually take over the space.

Later, in the summer, when *Aster sedifolius* has attained its full height (and been given brushwood support), the situation is different. Now it can cope with a mantle, say of scarlet nasturtiums, that looks marvellous scattered through or over the mauve quilt. But when frost has killed the nasturtiums and the aster has been cut down and cleaned up, you're back with your basal cushion of next year's shoots, and these are precious.

Helenium 'Moerheim Beauty' is also a member of the daisy family and a similar case. Its bronze daisies start flowering at 1m/3ft in late June. Sometime in August they should be given a dead-heading, cutting back to where a whole lot more flowering buds, lower down the stems, are already evident, awaiting their turn and prepared to provide a second surge of bloom. Few if any of the modern cultivars have this capacity for repetition, although their blooms are often a better shape. So its season is a long one, but you must then cut it down as low as you can to admit light to the green basal cushion of leaves that will take over next year. Don't allow any competition whatsoever near to these, but remember that they are very susceptible to slug damage. Any plant sharing space with this helenium must be really small. No camassias (and certainly not *Camassia leichtlinii* subsp. *suksdorfii* 'Electra') or *Leucojum aestivum* or long-leaved narcissus. Even the larger snowdrop cultivars, like *Galanthus* 'Atkinsii', will be too overpowering, though the wild snowdrop, *G. nivalis* unimproved, would be safe.

VARYING CIRCUMSTANCES

Each site, you must remember, is different, though the same plant may flourish under these varying circumstances. The 2m/6ft-tall, strongly growing Joe Pye weed, *Eupatorium purpureum* subsp. *maculatum* 'Atropurpureum', bears domes of purple blossom for a long summer season. It is a moisture lover and Beth Chatto grows it on the margin of one of her ponds in the company of other

▲ *No plant looks deader than a gunnera in winter but the space it releases is occupied by plants whose growing season will be completed before darkness descends: wood anemones (*A. nemorosa*), Lent lilies (*Narcissus pseudo-narcissus*), snakeshead fritillaries (*Fritillaria mele-agris*) and, later, but before the gunnera engulfs all else, self-sown spotted orchids (*Dactylorhiza fuchsii*).*

▼ *The vast leaves of* Gunnera manicata, *seen here in May when the compound flower head is conspicuous, continue to unfold into July.*

strongly growing moisture lovers. Even the big leaves of *Gunnera tinctoria* make suitable neighbours. In such a position the spring-flowering accompaniment would need to be something like a celandine, *Ranunculus ficaria*, in one cultivar or another; wood anemones would colonize, as would snakeshead fritillaries, *Fritillaria meleagris*.

At the back of our Long Border the context is different, although the eupatorium is just as happy there. Nothing would be able to survive actually in or under the clumps, as it would be unable to penetrate the dense roots and dormant eupatorium shoots. But sweet woodruff, *Galium* (once *Asperula*) *odoratum*, could run over the surface, its whorls of leaves a singularly bright green in spring while its heads of little cruciform flowers are dead white. Celandines could cohabit on top of the clumps as well, while in between clumps we run tulips, which look fine in a border setting but would be totally inappropriate on a pondside.

Colchicums are something of an exception. I mean the ones which flower in late summer and autumn but make their volum-inous, glossy leaves in spring. Many gardeners revile these, because they get in the way and look sleezy when dying off (don't we all?). But in March and April I think they look rather splendid.

Then, in late summer and autumn, the colchicums come to life again by flowering. Whatever you grow with them must not

◄◄ *The maidenhair fern,* Adiantum venustum, *makes a low but comely carpet of foliage year round, sometimes assuming rusty tints if the weather is cold. Through it colchicum leaves can penetrate in early spring (left). The leaves die off in May but the flowers in October (right) have the fern as a persisting background.*

▼ *The little* Narcissus *'Tête-à-tête', which spreads freely in our borders, is seen here in March, fitting comfortably into an association of dark-leaved celandine and emerging crocosmias.*

▶▲ *The lesser celandine,* Ranunculus ficaria, *has innumerable cultivars, the advantage of this one,*

'Brazen Hussy', which I found as a wilding in a nearby wood, being that its dark foliage sets off the brilliance of the flowers. They are at their best in March. Among the celandines can be seen the young pleated spears of Crocosmia 'Lucifer', which will take over later in the season, flowering in July–August. The celandine tubers remain in a state of dormancy throughout the summer. Like all celandines, 'Brazen Hussy' needs watching to prevent it taking over where it is unwanted.

▶▼ *The strong red colouring of* Crocosmia *'Lucifer' is more than welcome, but it does not last for very long. The seed heads are vaguely attractive.*

conceal their great moment. But I do disagree with the many gardeners who allow their colchicums to flower in a waste of bare soil or a bark blanket. That is negative and looks most unnatural. In nature, remember, they are most often in meadows and surrounded by grass. Hence one of their names, meadow saffron. I find the little maidenhair fern, *Adiantum venustum*, a most satisfactory companion, its carpeting growth being really light, and it is quite happy to be shaded on occasion. Beth Chatto grows colchicums through periwinkles, *Vinca minor*, in one variant or another. To keep the vinca low, it will need shearing back to ground level every or every other year. Take your opportunity when the colchicums are dormant. January or February would be a good time.

This is a technique to employ with periwinkles wherever they may be growing, as their main crop of flowers comes in early spring from ground level and too much stem and foliage above the ground spoils the display. We shear back in early February every other year.

SPACES BENEATH LATE PROTAGONISTS

We always hope that the shrubby *Clerodendrum bungei* will bring plenty of its upright, suckering stems unharmed through the winter. In that case you only have to tip them (at varying levels) the next spring and it will flower, with domes of deep pink buds opening to slightly lighter, scented flowers, starting early in August and continuing for nearly three months. It will put up with a good deal of shade and has large, dark, heart-shaped leaves, but in winter is entirely naked, so you can grow quite strong bulbs beneath it like the giant snowdrop, *Galanthus* 'Washfield Colesbourne', to be followed from late April onwards with Welsh poppies, orange or yellow, *Meconopsis cambrica*.

Most crocosmias (montbretias) flower from midsummer on, and are strong protagonists in the last months of the growing season, so we grow quite a few of them. One of the best known is the vigorous, 1.2m/4ft 'Lucifer', a very strong, pure shade of red. Actually, its flowering lasts for only three weeks at the outside, at the turn of July–August, so I don't believe in allowing it too much garden space. Ours are entirely colonized over the top of their corms by the celandine, *Ranunculus ficaria*, which I originally found as a sport in a nearby wood (now overgrown by brambles) and introduced to the garden because of its purple foliage, which makes an admirable background to its bright yellow flowers.

So I called it 'Brazen Hussy' (hussy was the old abbreviation for housewife and was used in the same pejorative sense as we do now). The name was suggested by a friend, Hugh Saunders, so I mustn't take the credit. As the carpet of celandines is dying off (though its tubers remain for future years), the crocosmia's spears push through.

'Brazen Hussy' flowers in March–April and in the same area I have the popular mini trumpet daffodil, *Narcissus* 'Tête-à-tête'. The name derives from its sometimes having two flowers, back to back, on a stem. Far more often, under garden conditions, where the bulbs are never able to get large, they come singly. At the time that 'Tête-à-tête' is flowering, in earliest spring, there is little movement from other perennials, so we allow it to spread freely (it self-sows) through many borders. Its bright yellow colouring shows up well even at a distance, so you will be able to see and enjoy it even at the back of a deep, one-sided border.

Another crocosmia that I find entertaining is called C. × *crocosmiiflora* 'Jackanapes'. Its small flowers are in keeping with a quite lowly height of 60cm/2ft, and they are in two distinct colours, bronze and orange. It is July-flowering. With this, I have a pink-flowered version of a blue scilla, *Scilla bifolia* 'Rosea', whose

◀ *The hardy* Begonia grandis *subsp.* evansiana *at the front of this border is planted for spring effect with the pure white* Allium neapolitanum. *This dies away completely as the begonia takes over. Behind is a Japanese anemone,* A. × hybrida *'September Charm', with a running habit that needs checking periodically. Behind these again, an invaluable hydrangea,* H. macrophylla *'Madame Emile Mouillère', which flowers from late June until the first frosts. The flowers are born in succession: as the early heads go over, remove them and more will develop on younger shoots. This is an ideal succession.*

flowering briefly fills a gap in spring. It is clump-forming, about 23cm/9in tall.

The crocosmia called C. × *crocosmiiflora* 'Solfatare' has apricot-coloured flowers and bronze leaves. It is highly regarded, but one of the weakest-growing of all. And the bronzer the leaves, the weaker it is. Still, one wants it. A long-flowering companion that I'm fond of is the little *Leucojum autumnale*. Only 23cm/9in or so tall, it produces a long succession of blush-white bells. The bulbs are surprisingly large and it is a tougher plant than it looks. Just around here I also have *Allium montanum*, whose ground-hugging leaves grow in intriguing swirls. The mauve flower heads appear in August. So while this is not so much a succession it is very much a partnership.

A rather surprisingly successful combination has *Begonia grandis* subsp. *evansiana* as the master plant. It is famed for its hardiness within a generally tender genus and its abundant pink flowers are borne in late summer and early autumn. Even if it is in full bloom, the first hint of a frost makes it shed all its blossom overnight. Never mind, it is an attractive plant for a semi-shaded, front-of-border position. Around it we have charming though actually aggressive *Allium neapolitanum*. It is one of those winter-green plants from the Mediterranean area, with bright green, lanky grass-leaves all through the winter, that finishes its growing season by flowering in May – domed heads of purest white flowers, no more than 30cm/1ft tall. It then becomes dormant till the following late autumn. If allowed to, it self-sows incontinently, but this is easily prevented. As soon as it is running to seed, you grab each clump between both hands and tug. Everything, flower stems and foliage, breaks cleanly away from the bulbs, which remain unharmed well below ground surface level.

Plant partnerships are a lot of fun, stretching your wits and encouraging you to experiment all the time. I will conclude where I started by repeating that whatever you use as an adjunct to your main display plant, the latter's growth and welfare must not be inhibited.

◀▲ *Anemone blanda*
Windflower
Height and spread:
12.5cm/5in
Hardy, sun or partial
shade
These anemones are ideal
plants to tuck into spring
spaces, making early car-
pets of blue, white or pink.
A. b. 'White Splendour',
which is more vigorous
than the other colours,

gets along famously
beneath deciduous Hor-
tensia hydrangeas and
in the temporarily bare
ground in front of *Cestrum
parqui*, loosely trained
against a sunny wall.

▼ *Eranthis hyemalis*
Winter aconite
Height: 8cm/3in
Spread: 5cm/2in
Hardy, light shade

Golden flowers in Febru-
ary, supported by a ruff
of green leaves. Good for
planting under trees or
shrubs if the soil is moist
enough. Among colonies
of hostas, it will form
drifts, completing its
growth by the end of April
and before the hostas are
shading the ground.

▼ *Erythronium* 'Pagoda'
Height: 44cm/18in
Spread: 20cm/8in
Hardy, best in part shade
Beneath deciduous
trees and among clump-
forming ferns is a good
place for this vigorous,

early-spring-flowering
bulb, but the soil should
never be too dry. One
parent is *E. tuolumnense*,
which is also bright
yellow. Once you get
erythroniums established,
they will multiply into

fat clumps with their own
offsets. That is, if they are
left undisturbed. I tend to
lose mine among other
plants in the mixed bor-
der, so I give them an
area to themselves
beneath *Cornus
alternifolia* 'Argentea'.

Galanthus nivalis
Common snowdrop
Height: 15cm/6in
Spread: 10cm/4in
Hardy, sun or partial shade
If we have deciduous trees
and shrubs, and even
perennials that are left
to get on with it, there
should be snowdrops
beneath. The fact that
the common snowdrop's
vigour is limited is a great
advantage when you don't
want an over vigorous
precursor.

Hyacinthus orientalis
Hyacinth
Height: 20–25cm/8–10in
Spread: 10–15cm/4–6in
Hardy, sun or light shade
Solid spires of very
fragrant flowers appear
in March. I love to have
hyacinths outside, in my
borders, where their scent

is wafted on the air. They
fill spaces around shrubs.
I buy the smallest grade
of bulb available, usually
from a wholesaler,
because the whoppers
look out of place.

▼ *Iris reticulata*
Height: 10–15cm/4–6in
Spread: 5–10cm/2–4in
Hardy, sun
A graceful little iris, with indigo-purple flowers in February, forming prolific clumps over a period (seen here with *Galanthus gracilis*). I interplant it with *G. nivalis* 'Tiny' in a space later occupied by cranesbills, such as

Geranium × *riversleaianum* 'Mavis Simpson', *G. wallichianum* 'Syabru' or *G.* 'Salome'.

▶ *Narcissus* 'Tête-à-tête'
Mini trumpet daffodil
Height: 15cm/6in
Spread: 5–10cm/2–4in
Hardy, sun
Small, February–March-flowering daffodils that can be fitted in almost

anywhere. The cheerful colouring of 'Tête-à-tête' shows up well even at a distance, so you will be able to see and enjoy it even at the back of a deep, one-sided border. I have it growing through dark-leaved celandines and in spaces where summer-flowering perennials follow on.

Ranunculus ficaria
'Brazen Hussy'
Lesser celandine
Height: 10cm/4in
Spread: 15cm/6in
Hardy, sun or partial shade
Makes carpets of purple-black foliage which are an admirable background to bright yellow flowers that open in sunshine during March and April. I plant this celandine with crocosmia, which pushes through bright green spears and takes over as the celandines are retiring below ground in early summer (the tubers remain for future years).

▼ *Scilla bithynica*
Turkish squill
Height: 10–15cm/4–6in
Spread: 8cm/3in
Hardy, sun or shade
This makes sheets of pale blue (sometime too pale and wan) in early spring. It completely took over large areas of Cherry (Captain Collingwood) Ingram's garden at Benenden in Kent, which was the origin of my

colonies. There it hob-nobbed with the magenta, spring-flowering *Cyclamen repandum*. I find it thrives beneath the low branches of *Magnolia* × *soulangeana* 'Lennei' and also among common male ferns, *Dryopteris filix-mas*, after their fronds have been cut down early in the new year. Snow-drops also grow here.

▲ *Tulipa sprengeri*
Height: 40cm/16in
Spread: 10cm/4in
Hardy, sun
The last of all the tulips in flower, with us this is at its peak usually in late

May. I grow it in a clump next to *Fuchsia* 'Genii', in the same space as snow-drops earlier in the year. This tulip species is also a charming accompaniment to bearded iris.

Spring and early-summer
BEDDING

Bedding plants provide a dazzling fix for gaps in a border's display, allowing us to change our mind and expect almost immediate satisfaction. Nothing wrong with that, surely?

The flexibility of bedding is what makes it exciting. It appeals to the showman element, the delight in a touch of panache that should be in each of us (but, alas, is often not). Bedding schemes can be formal, which is fine if well done and in the right setting. It is particularly effective on the garden front of Waddesdon Manor in Buckinghamshire, where a pattern of thousands of plants takes on a life of its own in cunningly arranged swirls. Often, bedding is crude and unimaginative – the 'open jam tart' syndrome, as my mother dubbed it. Circles, squares, triangles and kidney-shaped beds (a favourite) cut out of mown grass.

Or bedding can be informal, with plants integrated into the mixed border, which is the type of bedding that is fun and really suits our temperament and needs at Dixter. We sometimes bed out three times in a year in the same space. Some will say that it is extravagant – a favourite word of my mother's, said with the relish of deep disapproval and preceded, inevitably, by 'very'. Away with the kill-joys (not that she was, in most things).

By no means all of our bedding is integrated. We also include bedding-out areas that are designated solely for that purpose, but they fit comfortably into a setting that is only semi-formal and their contents are varied, by no means stereotyped.

The term bedding or bedding-out is currently unfashionable. This is a kind of snobbery and an attempt to boost the detractor's

▲ Tulips have many roles as bedding plants. Some are lifted and dried after flowering, but many remain in situ from year to year and are merely topped up to ensure they make a good show. When tulip foliage is dying, it isn't a nuisance like that of daffodils, but is easily absorbed by its neighbours. Here in the Barn Garden orange 'Ballerina' is mixed with red 'Dyanito' in the foreground. 'Queen of Sheba' reigns supreme at the back, merging with permanent plantings behind. Its thunder is stolen, just for a few days in late April, when Arum creticum flowers – a bright yellow spathe with upright spadix. Massed patches of wallflowers (Erysimum cheiri, syn. Cheiranthus cheiri) are bedded in contrasting colours.

ego. 'Cottage gardens' (however you may like to define them) are fashionable. There are plenty of temporary plants in them, so where do you draw the line? It's just a question of terminology.

'It's all a lot of work' is the commonest objection, but remember that we want the show to run on full throttle from April to October, not forgetting winter either.

THE CASE FOR BEDDING

The range of possible bedding combinations is mind-boggling, but let's get the disadvantages out of the way first. It entails a high workload, okay, but then look at the results. The inputs bring their own rewards.

It can look out of place if the right plants are not used, but that is just as true of perennials.

Bedding takes time to settle down and come into flower. If you rely too much on it, you have distinct 'lows' in the garden, such as when you are switching from spring to summer bedding. This is sometimes known as the June gap. I must at this point just mention a famous exception, the Buchart Gardens on Vancouver Island. Here the owner insisted on all the extensive bedding-out being in flower all the time. He wouldn't even accept a centrepiece of purple-leaved *Cordyline* because it wasn't flowering (nor ever would). 'Out with it,' he commanded. So all the bedding is raised out of sight, some, like *Schizanthus*, in pots, to be turned out when in full bloom, and some in the open ground from where, after a suitable drenching, the flowering plants are moved bodily. Even annuals like large-flowered zinnias, whose roots are said to be so sensitive to disturbance, are moved in full bloom. Rules, they say, are made to be broken and there is something in that. At the least, they are no more than guidelines and should be questioned, when you have the confidence to do so. Everything we do in the garden needs questioning, almost on a daily basis. It won't then go stale.

Within a mixed border, the lows generated by bedding that has not yet got going are mitigated and pass largely unnoticed because other more stable types of plant are having their fling. Then again, not all your bedding display gaps occur at the same time. Your changeovers are spread. When spring flowers, like forget-me-nots, are rooted out and replaced, there'll be bedded June-flowerers to catch our attention.

Turning now to the advantages of bedding, we should never underplay the fact that it is the icing on the cake, the jewellery on a garden's parure, vibrant with great colour combinations, full of *buzz*. And there's great flexibility and variety in what we can achieve, spring, summer and autumn, the later phase of which I am saving for the next chapter. We can and should experiment. When something turns out to be a mistake, it can be swept away at a stroke (something we can't so easily do with shrubs and trees) and forgotten; only the lesson remembered. (A photographic record might give us a laugh in future years.)

In a mixed border we want the bedding plants to gel with their surroundings. This can generally be achieved by allowing our principal bedding-plant grouping to explore a little beyond its official territory with a thread or two finding its way into and among its neighbours.

Continuity of interest is the forte of most bedding. In a central section of our Long Border where Weigela 'Florida Variegata' is an anchor plant with a long season of interest, a succession of temporary plantings shows the flexibility and variety we can achieve through the seasons.

▲▲ **In late April** the border's overall spring theme of forget-me-nots is enlivened with Lily-flowered 'White Triumphator' tulips making a display among clumps of foxglove foliage. The foxgloves need replanting at the turn of June–July and we harvest the tulip bulbs at the same time.

▲ **The second week of May** and the weigela is wreathed in scented flowers, pale blue Camassia cusickii is in flower and the forget-me-nots are hanging on. Allium foliage is well developed, with some buds showing. But the brilliant orange Siberian wallflower, Erysimum × marshallii (syn. E. × allionii), which has been highly visible for several weeks, is the jewel-

lery on the border's parure. This was sown the previous autumn and planted out from pots in March.

▲ **In early June**, just a few weeks later, the Siberian wallflower is still flowering and Digitalis purpurea Glittering Prizes Group has reached its full height next to the weigela. These will be replaced by dahlias and cannas in early July. There

are three alliums: at the front the pure white, early-flowering A. neapolitanum; the taller of the mauve-flowered is A. 'Globemaster', which clumps up rapidly; and the shorter is A. cristophii, which self-sows and retains its seed heads over a long season. A self-sown teazel has insinuated itself among the alliums. Will it stay or will it go?

▶ **Early September** *and
the teazel has had the
chop. We needed the space
for showy* Canna *'Erebus',
with salmon-pink flowers,
planted out in late June.*
Cosmos bipinnatus *'Son-
ata Pink' and* Ageratum
houstonianum *'Blue
Horizon', threaded through*
Allium cristophii, *have
been in flower since early
July. They will keep going
well into October.*

▲▲ *Single white arabis,
A. alpina subsp.* caucasica
*'Schneehaube' (Snowcap),
raised from seed sown the
previous spring, is a carpeter
that gives an opportunity
for two further bedding-out
schemes in the same season.
The arabis has short stems
and large, white blooms
from March into May,
making a perfect setting for
other early flowerers, such
as this* Narcissus 'Jetfire',
*which is deep yellow with
a light orange trumpet.*

▲ *Both the arabis and narcissus have finished flowering by the end of April, so
the site is clear for the next
brainwave! Here is an early-
flowering annual from
a March sowing (the brainwave was well planned):
the bright orange daisy,
Osteospermum hyoser-
oides, combined with blue
perennial* Triteleia laxa.

▶ *We plant out June–July-
flowering* Cynoglossum
amabile *in April or even
May from sowings over-
wintered under cold glass.
Autumn sowing produces
the best plants, as long as
they survive without damp-
ing off, but February–
March is an alternative,
producing plants that
should be in flower by the
end of June. I dote on the
truly sky-blue colouring
which sets off pot marigolds
a treat. Here* Calendula
officinalis 'Prince Orange',
*with double flower heads
and a tall (75cm/30in),
upright habit, makes
a lively companion, and
a few plants go a long way.
However, they are a little
too thin on the ground and
we need to increase the
ratio of orange to blue.*

THE RIGHT TIMING

Timing our sowings is of great importance, so that we have the results ready for where we shall want them to do their stuff at just the right moment. Naturally we'll not get it right all the time, but we mustn't be too ready to blame the weather when it was really our own silly fault. If we don't learn humility in this game, we never shall.

One of the most frequent mistakes is getting excited prematurely (and this also applies to gardeners who rely on buying bedding from garden centres). A lovely spell of early spring weather and off we go. But either our seedlings will hang around getting spoilt for weeks before their places are ready for them or they'll say, when we plant them out, 'I wasn't made for this; the ground's cold; the air's cold; what do you take me for?' They'll just sit, mutinous and miserable; zinnias, for instance. Or their leaves will turn bright yellow and take on that awful pinched look, as happens with *Ipomoea* 'Heavenly Blue'.

Quite apart from suiting the plant's needs (late sowing is generally safer than early, but not always; something like the pot marigold, *Calendula*, will romp away from an early sowing, but then we must be ready with its garden position so that it doesn't get spindly while waiting), we need to suit our own.

There is great flexibility here. If we have bedders that flower early in spring, we can replace with early-summer bedding and that, in its turn, by late-summer bedding which has been sown late, to perform at the right time. This will see us through until the first frost.

More often, the spring bedding will go on into the start of summer and we shall then be able to replace it with only one other display. Our sowing dates will be guided by this.

SPRING CARPETERS

Spring bedding can get into its stride as early as late March and it is worth remarking that to give old winter a final kick in the backside with great splashes of colour is tremendously invigorating. All right, we've been grateful to the snowdrops and the hellebores for tiding us over, but now we have the start of a feast that we've been pining for. Never mind how great the colour clashes that we perpetrate. The great thing at this early date is to have it – lots and lots of it set among the spring green of young foliage.

Seedling *Arabis alpina* subsp. *caucasica* 'Schneehaube' (Snowcap) makes a blinding white carpet of cruciferous blossom with single flowers. Some folk will prefer the double arabis, *A. a.* subsp. *caucasica* 'Flore Pleno', whose flowers are prettily rosette-shaped.

The plant is sterile, but easily raised from cuttings – a bunch of
three stems poked into the ground outside, in August, will allow
for failure if one or two of them should fail. The disadvantage as
I see it is that the plants are never as neat as those of the single.
Given the spare space, we can cut the singles hard back after
flowering and line them out (splitting if necessary) for the summer
but bedding with them again come the fall.

We can grow blue hyacinths among the arabis or the early red-
flowered *Tulipa eichleri*, which has beautiful central markings when
open to the sun. Or both, dead-heading the hyacinth if it finishes
earlier. Another possibility is to interplant with the Fosteriana

Group tulip 'Yellow Emperor', which is early, shortish and has enormous, pure yellow flowers when open wide to the sun. However, the leaves are very wide too, so we shall need to plant them comparatively sparsely if they are not to obliterate the arabis entirely. Another excellent arabis companion is the early-flowering Cyclamineus daffodil, *Narcissus* 'Jetfire'. Bright yellow with a pale orange trumpet. It would be hard to overpraise this cultivar, which never takes an off-year but always flowers prodigiously and has nothing coarse in its growth. I also like it in a permanent planting with the dwarf, magenta-pink *Bergenia stracheyi*, but that's a matter of taste – you might say bad taste. And I have a solitary yet telling clump of 'Jetfire' in front of white-flowered *Helleborus × nigercors*, whose flowering coincides.

Aubrieta makes another pleasing carpeter in April, often starting in March. From seed, I find the 'Royal Blue' strain, sown the previous June–July, does a satisfactory job although, of course, it is mauve, not blue. Until we get bored with them, we save plants from year to year, giving them the usual treatment: cut hard back after flowering, split and line out for the summer.

Tulips are good with that. Some people object to the gap between carpeter and tulip flowers, but that doesn't worry me a bit. We can, however, use tulip 'Prinses (Princess) Irene', which is short and early and in a weird mixture of apricot-orange overlaid with that bluish bloom that tulips go in for, making descriptions difficult.

The Lily-flowered tulip 'Ballerina' would also be suitable and it is one of our greatest favourites – a soft shade of orange but grading to rosy-red on the outside of the outer segments. How did it think of that? Fergus suggests *Tulipa eichleri*, which he loves.

Most polyanthus are early flowerers. Within the Crescendo Series we especially fancy *Primula* 'Crescendo Red'. Always go in for separate colours, however awkward to find. Polyanthus mixtures can be among the worst setters of teeth on edge. My teeth give me enough trouble without that. Imagine pink and puce mixed in with yellow and orange. For sourcing, we go to the publication called *The Seed Search*, which is improving every year and gives sources abroad as well as at home. There are also wholesalers who market separate colours where retailers have settled for the easy option (also accepted by the general public on the something of everything principle) of mixtures. And there is the internet.

Primula 'Crescendo Bright Red' would be a match for the early white Fosteriana tulip 'Purissima', but again remember that this has very broad leaves and should not be overdone. 'Crescendo Blue

Shades' (the centre of the flower is yellow) would team up with 'Yellow Emperor' tulips. A note of warning. If members of the primula family are grown in the same piece of ground year after year, they will go down to soil sickness (in the same way as roses do). We must think in terms of rotations. I love to grow bedding auriculas outside, in a reasonably shaded spot. Their especially delicious scent is wafted on the air. But we must remember that they are primulas. I shall remark that I have been written to by a New Zealander who declares that soil sickness, said to be caused, in part at least, by nematodes, is unknown there. Cause for emigration?

The bright yellow *Alyssum saxatile* is now *Aurinia saxatilis*. It is unashamed mustard yellow and can look rather awful with bright pink rock phloxes (but I shouldn't take even that for granted). Contrast it with an overplanting of the amazing bronze and yellow tulip 'Abu Hassan', which is available, although the *RHS Plant Finder* is weak on tulips. *Aurinia saxatilis* 'Citrina' is the polite lemon yellow alyssum. It is a bit weaker-growing but a good plant to use as a carpeter. We save our old plants after flowering, in the usual way.

April-flowering *Doronicum* for quite early bedding, 60cm–1m/ 2–3ft tall, are unusual but admirable. It is easiest to raise a fresh batch annually, grown from summer-sown seed. Their cheerful yellow daisies bleach badly in strong sunlight, so they are best in light shade, perhaps interplanted with white tulips. Ask for *D. caucasicum* 'Magnificum' or *D. orientale* 'Magnificum' if necessary from a wholesaler. It won't cost a lot. If we cut the doronicums down and line them out after flowering, we always seem to sustain a good many losses. That may just be us.

Tulips over forget-me-nots (it is less cumbersome to call these myosotis, which means a mouse's ear) is traditional, but it works as well as ever. Most of the myosotis seed strains available make compact, dumpy plants. I far prefer the more natural, freely branching kinds, which we have had for as long as I can remember. They self-sow, of course, so supplies are always to hand. The dumpy kinds, if grown on from seed, year after year, will automatically revert to the free-and-easy style.

WALLFLOWERS WITH BULBS

And so we reach May, with wallflowers among the principals. They have undergone tiresome name changes, *Cheiranthus* disappearing in favour of *Erysimum*, but few of the catalogues take any notice of this. The traditional bedding wallflower, still known as *Cheiranthus*

▲ *Early-flowering Polyanthus 'Rainbow Blue' and the Fosteriana Group tulip 'Yellow Emperor' make a good team as far as timing is concerned, but the blue background is too sulky for my taste, such a lively tulip deserving more vibrant company. With wide leaves, the tulip needs to be well spaced so as not to obliterate its partner.*

▶ *It makes a change to use a spring-flowering perennial as a bedding plant, especially one that is happy with a bit of shade, as it might be from overhead trees. Leopard's bane grows excessively tall in the wild, but there are dwarf selections, such as Doronicum orientale 'Magnificum' (syn. D. caucasicum 'Magnificum'), that make good bedders, here with yellow tulips. We sow the seed in April to flower the following year, lining them out for the summer.*

▶▶ *Of the two very distinct cultivars of variegated Lunaria annua, the biennial honesty as we call it, or money flower in the USA, I prefer L. a. 'Variegata'. This is the one with disorganized variegation and mauve flowers. Being a self-sower with a tendency to revert to plain green, it needs some control (see page 149), but then makes a great companion to spring bedding and is charming mixed in with the Lily-flowered Tulipa 'China Pink'.*

▼ Globes of Allium hollandicum *'Purple Sensation'* rising above the biennial Campanula patula *was the original, all-mauve-and-purple scheme for this bed in the Solar Garden. Although self-sown Welsh poppies and mauve honesty pepped it up a bit, it still seemed tame, until we introduced a few rivulets of dazzling orange Siberian wallflowers, Erysimum* × marshallii. *The effect was electrifying, but by no means overpowering.*

▶ *The traditional bedding wallflower,* Erysimum cheiri *but still known as* Cheiranthus cheiri, *generally reaches a peak with us in early May, whereas mauve* Erysimum linifolium *comes a couple of weeks later and makes an ideal match for my favourite latest tulip 'Dillenburg'. This is orange but has a pink flush on the outside of the outer segments. Timing of wallflower sowings is a matter of experiment. We sow in early July – any earlier and the plants flower prematurely in the same year and are weakened.*

cheiri (the ch should be pronounced as k but the name is often spoken as Cheeryanthus cheeryi, the ch soft), generally reaches a peak in May. It should be mentioned that old plants may survive for a good number of years, if left somewhere (as in a wall or hedge bottom) undisturbed. These may start to flower as early as December. In course of time they become riddled with virus disease (which they pass on to *Lunaria annua* with dire effect), and if they started out bronze, they will become stripy in bronze and yellow, their vigour noticeably reduced. I don't worry.

Wallflowers are by nature scrawny plants, having nothing to boast about in terms of plant shape. If interplanted with other bedders, their scrawniness is emphasized, as they lean this way and that. I believe in planting them in massed patches. The companion plant can either make its own undiluted patch in front of or behind the wallflowers or you can leave channels between wallflower patches, in which to plant bulbs. The orange tulip 'Dillenburg', having a pinkish-red flush on the outside, is especially suitable, because so late flowering. For the same reason it combines well with the mauve *Erysimum linifolium*, a cushion-forming plant best sown in late summer to flower the following May. The wonderful Lily-flowered 'Queen of Sheba' is much the same colour as wallflower 'Fire King', though infinitely more subtle both inside the bloom and out. It has a long flowering season and is irresistible.

If a good source for plump wallflower plants can be found, so much the better. They do exist. But there's little money in selling wallflower plants and most often you will be buying miserable specimens. Far better to grow our own, if the space can be found. We sow into a drill outside in early July, making sure beforehand that there is plenty of moisture in the soil. If necessary, we water the bottom of the drill before sowing. Then we row out the seedlings as soon as large enough to handle, say 20cm/8in apart, but that will depend on how vigorous a strain we are growing. We move to where they will flower in the autumn, when their places have been made vacant.

There is no scent comparable to a wallflower's. Stand on top of a sea cliff in which they are naturalized and the upward draught will bring it to you in wonderful gusts. But the Siberian wallflower, which flowers a bit later, is also deliciously scented, although quite differently. The plant is different, too, not being woody. It will often self-sow, where it can be allowed to. Its colouring is the brightest, clearest orange imaginable. Great stuff, but many gardeners quail

A succession planting in the Barn Garden has biennial clary, Salvia sclarea var. turkestaniana, as the main protagonist.

▲ **In May** Allium hollandicum 'Purple Sensation' is the focus while the salvia takes time to get its act together. Like many of its tribe, this allium has foliage that is withering by the time it flowers, but this is well hidden by the salvia's wrinkled leaves.

▶ ▲ **By the end of June** Salvia sclarea var. turkestanica is flowering at its full height of 2m/6ft and the alliums have retired into discreet aestivation, leaving only their attractive green seed heads. Self-sown, magenta-flowered Lychnis coronaria has infiltrated and, along with the sage, will have run out of steam and can be thrown out in late July to make way for a bedding display that takes us into autumn. We harvest the allium bulbs at the same time.

before it and seek out gentrified strains lacking that vitalizing punch.

Mind you, a little goes a long way as the true Siberian shows up vividly at a distance. Fergus did a rather polite area (a large area) of bedding with the biennial *Campanula patula*, which is campanula blue, and the globes of *Allium hollandicum* 'Purple Sensation' rising above it. I forced him (one occasion where I had my way against his instincts) to work in a few meandering rivulets of Siberian wallflowers. The way they pepped that bedding up was electrifying. I love them scattered as small, strung-out incidents along the length of the Long Border, repeated evenly enough to show the intention but never hitting you over the head (or eyes) with a sledgehammer.

EARLY-SUMMER HIGHS

Turning to early-summer bedding, we are threatened with being plunged into the dreaded June gap, which need not exist at all. A gap somewhere is inevitable, when a changeover is made. But gaps can be diluted in a mixed border, by neighbouring plants that are at their peak.

Take a popular sage, *Salvia sclarea*, often found with *turkestan-*

iana tacked on. This is a great self-sower but we raise and bed out individually into the middle reaches of a border, interplanted with the May-flowering *Allium hollandicum* 'Purple Sensation', which carries striking purple globes of blossom at 1m/3ft, before the salvias have attained their full height. The sage flowers at 2m/6ft in June–July. They are mauve, most of their colour coming from bracts. By then the alliums will be totally engulfed, but will have done flowering and their bulbs can be harvested when the sage has itself run out of steam and will make way for a late-summer and autumn bedding display, which is described in the next chapter.

Cornflowers, *Centaurea cyanus,* can be had in a whole range of different colours, but I much prefer a traditional rich blue. True blues are rare enough and we don't want to neglect them. They'll make big plants from an autumn sowing that will flower at 1.5m/5ft and there's an area in our Long Border where we space the plants out widely, having raised them in quite large pots and planted out in early spring.

The problem always is to get the timing of our sowing right. They germinate rather quickly and, if sown too early, will run up to flower in the autumn, which is hopeless. Correct timing will

A succession in the Long Border reaches a peak in May and June with lupins, Lupinus polyphyllus, grown as biennials, but the planting also works hard in other seasons.

▲ **In April** we like tulips with our lupins. Here red T. 'Apeldoorn' looks striking with the fresh foliage of lupins that were planted out in November. We sow two colours that will associate well, ringing the changes from year to year.

▶▲ **In May** the lupins are flowering – and arouse a buzz of delight from me as much as from the bees. In this oblique view of the border, the background includes the large-flowered Clematis 'Lasurstern' which has engulfed its supporting peastick palisade, our old friend and anchor Euonymus fortunei 'Silver Queen', behind aquilegias, and right at the back Clematis recta 'Purpurea' with its support still visible. To stake or not to stake is a question we aim to avoid with the lupins.

▶▼ **Early July** sees Fergus digging up and throwing away the lupins. The tulips are harvested at the same time and dried off. Note the dwarf bamboo, Pleioblastus viridistriatus, on the right.

▶▶▼ **The high summer display** goes on into autumn, the lupins having been replaced in July by perennial Rudbeckia fulgida var. speciosa grown as a biennial. Further along the border are cannas and dahlias that were also introduced at this stage. Now, at the beginning of October, the border is still full of colour, with anchoring Pleioblastus viridistriatus and Euonymus fortunei 'Silver Queen' glowing in the autumnal light. By the end of November all the summer bedding will have been cleared away. We aim to do this and to replant next year's bulbs and bedding in a series of swoops.

vary according to the climate where you live and to the weather in each year. First week in October is often right for me. So long as the seedlings don't threaten to bolt, they should be potted on whenever they look as though they could benefit from it. In a cold frame they'll keep on growing all winter to be finished in 2-litre pots before planting out (or standing the pots outside the porch). They'll need staking. Spring sowings will flower a bit later, on smaller plants.

The one great irritation with cornflowers is that the flowers die off individually to a horrid bleached non-colour and really need dead-heading every other day, which is unlikely to be undertaken. But they have a long flowering season from late May.

Herbaceous lupins of the *Lupinus polyphyllus* type make a wonderful show in May and take us into June. Their peppery fragrance is all their own. A point that makes them unique is that while the spike is vertical, the whorls of blossom that compose it are horizontal. In a mixed border they are awkward to handle because they look so unappetising after flowering, invariably succumbing to powdery mildew. Neither can you cut them down, as you can Oriental poppies.

We find the best policy is simply to treat them as biennials, sowing in July. Normally we go for single colour strains, two of each that we think will combine interestingly in a border setting. The seedlings are lined out, keeping the two colours separate. They often flower a little the first autumn and any rogues can be thrown out.

We plant where they are to flower, in late autumn, alternating the two colours, and interplant with tall, single-colour tulips (red is good). The young lupin foliage makes an ideal background for the bulbs. Whether to stake the lupins in May, when they run up to flower, is always a question. Generally we don't and hope to get away with it, but are sometimes caught out by a high wind while they are actually in flower. Still …

The display will be over before the end of June. We rip the lupins out and chuck them. The tulips are harvested. Then over to the next excitement – dahlias, cannas, bananas or whatever. So that piece of ground works hard for us, wherever it may be, the position varying in different years.

Ammi majus is a brilliant annual/biennial. It is a typical umbellifer with a branching inflorescence of purest white, cow-parsley-style flowers. It is not quite winter-hardy. Sown in early autumn (the fresher the seed, the better the germination, as with many

umbellifers), the seedlings are potted individually and over-wintered in a cold frame. We plant them out in their flowering sites in early April. They will then rise to 2m/6ft and can be used with blue larkspurs in front of them, in the centre or back of a one-sided mixed border. The larkspurs' early treatment will be the same. If you can find one called 'Blue Cloud', which is as near to the wilding as you will get, that is ideal. Sown in spring, ammi will flower at 75cm/30in, and that is useful too, say with ladybird poppies.

POPPIES FOR MONTHS

This ladybird poppy, strictly speaking *Papaver commutatum* 'Ladybird', is crimson with a large, black spot at the base of the petals. We often plant it along the entire length of a double-sided, fairly narrow border, where it ties in with any of the mixed ingredients that it happens to pass. It can be sown in the autumn or at any time from February to June, its flowering time varying accordingly. Just experiment. Here are some suggestions:

1 With traditional blue love-in-a-mist, *Nigella damascena* 'Miss Jekyll', itself highly flexible. It self-sows like crazy, but we get the best plants by sowing under cold glass and potting off seedlings individually.

2 Again with blue, *Cynoglossum amabile*, making sure that we get a pure blue strain. It may be called something like 'Firmament'. Names keep changing but will clearly indicate the colour to be expected, and this must be blue. We can get large plants of the cynoglossum from an early-autumn sowing, but sometimes find them tricky to overwinter, in which case February on will do.

3 Still on the red and blue theme, with *Anchusa capensis*, an annual species, no more than 30cm/1ft tall and just about as intense a shade of pure blue as you will find.

4 With the woolly-felted leaves and discreet whitish sage flowers of *Salvia aethiopis* (seen wild on rather impoverished, disturbed soils, often by new roadsides, in central Europe), taller than the poppy but of open texture.

5 With Canterbury bells, *Campanula medium*. The traditional kinds are biennial and flower in June. Pink Canterburys are not suitable. We go for a blue or purple strain.

6 Finally with that delightful annual, *Omphalodes linifolia*, which self-sows on light soils but gives more predictable results under controlled conditions, sown in autumn (a bit dicey) or in early spring. About 30cm/1ft tall, the leaves are grey, the flower spikes white.

▼ We are extremely fond of the annual poppy, Papaver commutatum 'Ladybird', and thread it through long sections of our borders. Here it is at the end of May with Gladiolus communis subsp. byzantinus which remains in the ground and multiplies rapidly.

▶ Papaver commutatum is threading a passage through Euphorbia × martini, the brilliant lime-green spurge with a reddish-brown eye that I like with bright tulips earlier in the year. This is liable to flower in any season, but such generosity wears it out and, after three years, it is best to replace old plants. We propagate from leafy cuttings and bed these out from pots.

▲ Dianthus 'Rainbow Loveliness' with ragged flowers is a favourite pink on account of its syrup-sweet airborne scent. The timing of sowings is tricky but worth the effort. We save seed from year to year so as to have some control over the colour. Here in June the dianthus are growing with soft yellow Aquilegia chrysantha and a tall, pink columbine.

▶ Biennial foxgloves derived from our native Digitalis purpurea are at their best in June. This soft peach selection, D.p. 'Sutton's Apricot', would soothe the nerves of the most determined hater of pink-purple foxgloves as seen in the wild. These finish flowering by early July and are replaced with summer bedding that carries us forward until the first frosts.

MORE TEAMS IN JUNE

A range of *Dianthus* will flower in June – it is their principal month – from a sowing made the previous year. One of my favourites is the strain known as 'Rainbow Loveliness', derived from *D. superbus*, which you see wild in the Alps. It has a syrup-sweet scent which meets you on the air. Unless grown well, the plants are horribly spindly things, making no impact. This happens if they are sown prematurely and flowering is attempted before the winter. To be safe, we sow in early September (correct timing can never be guaranteed) and pot the seedlings individually to overwinter under cold glass. We plant out in April. The fair-sized flowers are fimbriated, which is to say that the petals are deeply cut, making a ragged fringe. The colour range is from white, through pink to quite a deep purplish-pink shade. I like a strain with plenty of the last and not too many wishy-washy ones. I always save my own seed (it ripens quickly) and take it from dark-flowered plants. It is

then sown almost immediately and will flower the following June.

The many strains of *Dianthus chinensis* offer a tremendous range of long-flowering, quite large-flowered dianthus, though they have no scent. On the trial ground at Harlow Carr I particularly noted the Princess, Ideal and Telstar Series, often available in separate colours from Moles Seeds. They include pure reds.

Many of the traditional June-flowering pinks derive from *Dianthus plumarius*. They have grey foliage and are sweetly scented. From a June sowing one year, of the 'Sonata Pink' strain, for instance, we line out the seedlings to grow on and they make large plants by the autumn. They are best planted before the new year, into their flowering positions. If their places are not ready for them, they have to wait till late winter or earliest spring.

There was an aquilegia (columbine) trial at Wisley which gave me the idea of using one called 'Mellow Yellow' solely as a foliage plant, early on. The flowers are no great shakes.

Again, with aquilegias, I would always go for single colour strains or species. *Aquilegia chrysantha*, a wilding from the USA, is pure, rather pale yellow, with spurs as long as you will find, and about 1m/3ft tall. A little shorter is *A.* (Songbird Series) 'Blue Bird'. We are putting these two together with the globes of *Allium hollandicum* rising above them. You can also plant tulips among aquilegias to give slightly earlier interest.

Rather a good team in June is a white strain of sweet rocket, *Hesperis matronalis*, behind (as it is considerably the taller) the vivid orange daisy, *Anthemis sancti-johannis*, which, as its name indicates, flowers on (and around) St John's Day, 24 June. Both are sown in late summer. The hesperis is lined out and moved to where it will flower, in autumn. The anthemis hates root disturbance in autumn, as it is about to rest, so we grow that in pots but plant it out in autumn without disturbing its roots. For an earlier diplay, we interplant both parties with tulips.

We interplant foxgloves with tulips, too, followed by patches of wallflowers. These are the biennial *Digitalis purpurea*, but we vary the colour strain used in different years: white, apricot or a mixture that we fancy. Foxgloves rise to 2m/6ft, so they are planted well back from any one-sided border's margin. The traditional one-sided foxglove spikes will nearly always face their flowers towards you if you are positioned on the side that receives most light, so there is no need to bother about strains that are recommended because flowers are borne all round the spike.

Bedding is fun – and the fun continues in the next chapter.

▼ Ammi majus
Bishops' flower
Height: 1–2m/3–6ft
Spread: 45cm/18in
Annual or biennial, sun
Pure white umbels with a
wonderful lightness have
quite a prolonged early-
summer flowering season,
making an effective foil for
the bright colours of other
annuals. Height is vari-
able: from a spring sow-
ing not more than 1m/3ft
but twice that height
from an autumn sowing
and brought on in pots.
Seed needs to be fresh.

▲ Arabis alpina subsp.
caucasica 'Schneehaube'
Snowcap arabis
Height: 15cm/6in
Spread: 50cm/20in
Hardy, sun

A vigorous, mat-forming
perennial, this makes a
white carpet in late
spring that sets off
hyacinths, early tulips
and narcissus. We sow

seed in a cold frame the
previous summer and
plant out when and where
the flowering positions
are ready.

Campanula persicifolia
Peach-leaved bellflower
Height: 75cm/30in
Spread: 10cm/4in
Hardy, sun
Either 'blue' or white, this
is an old-time cottage
garden favourite, a perennial, making a dense mat
of basal leaf rosettes. The
denser the carpet of foliage becomes, the fewer
there'll be of flowering
stems. We give individual
treatment to the rosettes,
lining them out in a spare
bit of ground to become
large and prosperous dur-
ing the summer. In the
autumn we bed them out,
sometimes with later-
flowering Dutch iris bulbs.
C. latiloba is similar, its
flowers borne closer
to the main stem. The
unusual rosy-mauve
'Hidcote Amethyst' is
a popular variant.

▲ Centaurea cyanus
Cornflower
Height: 1.5m/5ft (less if
spring-sown)
Spread: 45cm/18in
Hardy, sun
Traditional, rich blue-
flowered annual corn-
flowers, such as 'Blue Boy'
or 'Blue Diadem', have
a long flowering season
from late May. They make
big plants (you'll have
to stake them) from an
autumn sowing in quite
large pots and planted
out in early spring. Spring
sowings will flower a bit
later, on smaller plants.
Dead-head every other
day, if possible.

▼ Cynoglossum amabile
'Firmament'
Chinese forget-me-not
Height: 60cm/2ft
Spread: 30cm/1ft
Hardy, sun
Annual or biennial bushy
plant with light but bright
blue flowers from early
summer onwards. We
can get large plants of
the cynoglossum from an
early autumn sowing, but
sometimes find them
tricky to overwinter, in
which case February on
will do. We grow these

with blue lyme grass,
Leymus arenarius, and
with ladybird poppies,
Papaver commutatum, or
pot marigolds, *Calendula
officinalis*, for exciting
displays.

Doronicum orientale
'Magnificum'
Leopard's bane
Height: 75cm–1m/30in–3ft
Spread: 1m/3ft
Hardy, light shade
We raise April-flowering
Doronicum annually from
summer-sown seed. The

cheerful yellow daisies
are good among decidu-
ous shrubs, interplanted
with white or yellow tulips.
We cut the doronicums
down and line them out
after flowering, but we
always need to sow fresh
seed, additionally, in July.

▲ *Lupinus polyphyllus*
Herbaceous lupin or
lupine
Height: 1.2m/4ft
Spread: 60cm/2ft
Hardy, acid soil, sun
Herbaceous, clump-
forming lupins are early
on the move and already

showing young growth in
February. Hence the need
to establish them in their
flowering sites by the
previous autumn. We
sow single colour strains
in July. The seedlings are
lined out, keeping the
colours separate. They

often flower a little the
first autumn and any
rogues can be thrown
out. The young lupin
foliage makes an ideal
background for tulips.
When the display is over,
we rip the lupins out and
chuck them.

▶ *Myosotis*
Forget-me-not
Height: 40cm/16in
Spread: 60cm/2ft
Hardy, sun or shade
First of the biennials to
flower, the forget-me-nots
have a long season, form-
ing a running theme
through our borders in
April and up to the very
end of May. We use them
in a traditional way as
carpeters for tulips (here
'Prinses Irene'), but with
the bulbs in relaxed
rather than strict form-
ation. Gardeners seldom
buy seed, as old myosotis
plants shed seeds that
germinate like weeds. If
you need to acquire seed,
go for 'Royal Blue'.

**◀ *Nigella damascena*
'Miss Jekyll'**
Love-in-a-mist
Height: 38cm/15in
Spread: 23cm/9in
Hardy, sun or light shade
Blue flowers with filigree-
like appendages in late
spring and early summer,
followed by inflated seed
pods. An annual, it self-
sows like crazy but should
be thinned or potted up.
We get the best plants by
sowing under cold glass
and potting off seedlings
individually. *N. hispanica*
is an arresting, slightly
later-flowering alternative,
dark-centred and a little
sinister, but always
attracting attention.

***Papaver commutatum*
'Ladybird'**
Annual poppy
Height: 45cm/18in
Spread: up to 60cm/2ft
Hardy annual, sun
The annual poppy, which
I like to call the ladybird
poppy (ladybug, to
Americans), is of a deep
crimson colouring, with a

large, black blotch at the
base of each petal – red
and black is smart. We
grow from seed each year
in the autumn and from
February to June, its
flowering time varying
accordingly. We plant
it out lavishly to thread
through schemes that
need livening up. I've
never met anyone who
wasn't thrilled by them.
Other poppies or near
poppies (eschscholzias)
are also easily organized.

Salvia aethiopis
Sage
Height: 1m/3ft
Spread: 60cm/2ft
Hardy, sun
A monocarpic sage, with
woolly leaves that make
attractive rosettes before
it runs up to flower.
Stately but open-textured
and elegant, the flowers
whitish, this is a good
companion to ladybird
poppies.

▼ *Viola* Penny Series
Height: 10cm/4in
Spread: 15cm/6in
Hardy, sun but plenty of
moisture
There are some real
charmers among the little
violas, like 'Penny Blue',
'Penny Orange' and
'Penny Yellow'. They have
a quite amazingly long
flowering season in
spring and early summer,
and are scented on the
air. Sow seed in late
summer; choose a cool,
shady place outside for
the seed pots, moving
them into good light after
germination. Prick them
out in the usual way.

Summer
BEDDING
into autumn

Bedding continues the long season of display and interest, providing the final touches of make-up. It can be as light or as heavy as suits our needs. But it does need thought if it is to be done well.

◄ Flat-leaved parsley is best for flavour, but a strain with curls is a smashing bedding plant, sown in April for planting out in early August. Petroselinum crispum 'Bravour' has frilly leaves, closely packed, and is a particularly vivid shade of green. It contrasts excitingly with the bright orange dwarf marigold, Tagetes patula 'Disco Orange', which has a free habit and good, dark foliage. Verbena 'Homestead Purple' is investigating among the parsley and the little Zinnia 'Chippendale' behind.

What is the brightest, freshest green you can think of in August, when most greens are heavy and tarnished? Parsley, of course. Get yourself flat-leaved parsley to eat, but a really frilly, crimped one for display. If we then interplant it with the dwarf, single-flowered marigold, *Tagetes patula* 'Disco Orange', we'll realize that each is necessary to the other. We might thread a few bright purple bedding verbenas among them, not the clumpy kind but the exploring 'Homestead Purple' that is kept going from year to year by taking autumn cuttings. These names may change, but you get the idea.

Another bright green foliage bedder that keeps on improving for many months, eventually making a narrow, 1.8m/5¾ft column of needle-leaves is the tender *Eupatorium capillifolium*. At the front of a one-sided bed with an old cow shed, the hovel, behind it, I bedded out vividly coloured coleus (*Solenostemon*) hybrids, grown from seed and not bedded till early July, when the nights were reliably warm. On the hovel's wall is the yellow-leaved ivy, *Hedera helix* 'Buttercup'. But between coleus and ivy we planted a ribbon of the eupatorium and it made an essential break to an otherwise indigestible Joseph's coat of colour.

Solenostemon, better known as *Coleus* hybrids, are generally grown as cool house pot plants, but make a great show in the garden, given the chance, until the first frosts. We grow three

The border in front of the hovel has a permanent backdrop of Hedera helix 'Buttercup' climbing on the wall and on to its roof. A spot facing northwest is perfect for this ivy, which needs enough light to remain yellow, yet will scorch in blazing sun. The bedding in front of it, chosen to suit the cool position and afternoon sunlight, varies from year to year.

▲ *The coleus show gets going in early August and lasts well into October. We grow Solenostemon hybrids from mixed seed, giving them enough space and nourishment to make*

shapely plants. We sort them out by colour and markings before planting out in July. Here they have a light curtain of Eupatorium capillifolium as a break between them and the ivy on the wall. This green bedder retains its bright colouring right into October, when it is rare to find such freshness.

▶ *The same border but another year: Cleome pungens 'Pink Queen', the spider flower, can look like a shrub if well grown without a check and it flowers for two or three months. In front is our favourite Ageratum houstonianum 'Blue Horizon'.*

mixed strains from seed. They hate cold in the early stages and we haven't much heat on offer anyway, so we sow in May, using cold frames throughout, and have the plants ready to plant out from pots in early July. I should remind you that our cold frames are of no standard pattern apart from the use of Dutch lights as glazing. The sides of the frames are solid – wood, concrete blocks or bricks – so the frames retain their day heat through much of the night. If frost threatens, we cover them with lengths of hessian, which Americans call burlap.

Fergus brings all those coleus that look reasonable (any plain or unpleasant ones are discarded forthwith) to stand on the paving in front of the bed to be filled and I arrange them in groups of similar colouring and markings; then decide which groups will look nice next to which. They are then placed and planted. The show really gets going in early August and lasts well into October. A fall in temperature at that stage, short of freezing, doesn't affect them.

THE LATE SHOW

The last attitude you should take is to think the show is over when you return from an August holiday. If you live in a frost hollow and expect to get clobbered before September is out, I can only say, rather unsympathetically, that as a gardener you should have thought of that before you decided on where to settle.

Once spiny-stemmed cleomes start flowering, only the cold weather of late autumn will stop them. We sow in the second half of April. Their range of colours – pink, white and purple – are all compatible, so a mixture is okay but I generally concentrate on the white 'Helen Campbell', because it can be used in a range of contexts, whereas the pink (which has a touch of mauve in it) is quite a difficult shade when near to yellow, orange or red. Cleomes never want to be checked in their growth and they should never be allowed to become pot-bound. Given this attention, they will make large, base-branching plants of which you can be proud. They even look like shrubs. The growth of their flowering spikes is indefinite. One slight disadvantage is that in hot sunshine the flowers go limp. And their botanical name, *Cleome pungens*, gives away the fact that the plants have a strong, not altogether pleasant aroma. Nothing to make a fuss about. They also have a pair of spiny, green stipules at the base of each leaf. You'll soon find out about that.

Cleome pungens 'Helen Campbell' may grow 1.3m/4¼ft tall and looks good in front of the brilliant orange, zinnia-like *Tithonia*

▲ Giant dahlia-flowered zinnias need a warm summer to give of their best, which will be around the middle of September from an early-May sowing. These zinnias are flat-petalled and seen here in a mixture. As a dark back-ground we grow Cercis canadensis *'Forest Pansy' entirely for its red-purple foliage, pruning it hard each spring to achieve the desired effect. Behind that is the tall reed grass,* Arundo donax. *At the front of the border is an agave,* A. americana *'Mediopicta Alba', bedded out to add a touch of gravitas.*

rotundifolia 'Torch'. Tithonias also make an effective backdrop to a display of large, dahlia-flowered zinnias. These are especial favourites with Fergus and me and we were delighted that a trial of zinnias at Wisley made such a wonderful band of colour through-out September. Giant double zinnias are a speciality of the German firm of Benary, which breeds them in separate colours, so that you can make your own choice of which to put together. As yet, they are not well selected and pretty uneven, but that is sure to improve. Don't make the mistake of growing the strains, sometimes called chrysanthemum-flowered, whose rays are rolled back at the mar-gins. Miserable things. Large-flowered zinnias like heat and, while good in the south of England, especially after a summery summer, they are not much use in the north, where the tougher, small-flowered kinds are successful. This problem is unlikely to be met in most parts of the USA, where summer heat is perfectly adequate for any zinnias.

Grow the Profusion Series, which are not much more than 30cm/1ft tall. 'Profusion White' is unexpectedly pleasing (some-how one doesn't quite expect a white zinnia to have much going for it). But the best is 'Profusion Orange'. You'll have to go to a wholesaler for these separate colour strains. *Zinnia linifolia* is effective *en masse*.

GOOD MARIGOLDS

Marigolds – the various *Tagetes* – have a bad name with the snooty section of our public, who simply haven't bothered to sort out the good from the disgusting. Marigolds that have been bred to have large flowers on dwarf plants look terrible, being entirely without grace or personality, but they are, after all, easily avoided.

Marigolds have an outstandingly long flowering season, which is surely heavily in their favour. A large-flowered so-called African type (all came originally from Mexico and Central America), said to derive from *Tagetes erecta*, is an excellent garden plant if it grows 1m/3ft tall and shows plenty of its pinnate foliage between the flowers. F1 Toreador was a favourite with me but has been dropped. The best of this type currently is the Jubilee strain, which are tall enough to have a presence. The darker orange strains are a lot more powerful than the pale orange.

These marigolds look handsome with an occasional break among them of *Kochia* now *Bassia scoparia*, which is cone-shaped to 80cm/32in and a very bright green. Often called burning bush, it turns magenta before dying in autumn. This can be a little

disconcerting. There is a seed strain called 'Evergreen', but it isn't, and changes to magenta like the others.

Most of the smaller-flowered marigolds, called French, derive from *Tagetes patula*. The double-flowered kinds are usually rather horrid, but there are some excellent singles, like the dwarf 'Disco Orange' and the bright yellow 'Suzie Wong' (apart from anything else, how can one resist the name itself?). 'Cinnabar' was a dwarf bronze single with a very thin, orange rim. I have saved my own seed over many years, always taking it from the tallest plants, so that I now have what I consider to be a very presentable tallish strain. 'Striped Marvel' alternates bronze and orange striping that radiates from the centre of a single bloom and grows on a tallish plant. I like that. Each to his own. You may dislike all my likes, but you should certainly not dismiss all marigolds.

RUNNING THEMES

Annual rudbeckias (they sometimes survive the winter and flower a second year) are a mainstay from early July on. When I first saw *Rudbeckia hirta* 'Toto' on the Wisley trial ground, I thought what a horrible travesty – bright yellow with a black disc, but so dwarf and dumpy. However, it improved as its long season went on, the plants getting taller to 30 or 40cm/1ft or 16in, and varying a little in height from plant to plant. We find it excellent for threading through other low-growing plants, not necessarily annuals, and creating rivulets, the spacing varying in a natural sort of way.

I shouldn't have expected to like double rudbeckias, but was bowled over by the *R. hirta* Cherokee Sunset Group, in varying shades (all within the same fair-sized flower) of bronze. You certainly need to keep an open mind in this game. *Rudbeckia amplexicaulis* is completely different from one's normal conception of a rudbeckia, 1m/3ft tall, bushy and perfectly smooth in all its parts (most are rough-textured). Quite small yellow and black flowers but hosts of them. No one except for inveterate haters of yellow could fail to be taken by it.

Besides 'Toto', which we run through other plantings (we like it with the blue, upright *Nepeta nervosa*), the larger-growing and perennial *Rudbeckia fulgida* var. *speciosa* is excellent for the same purpose. We either introduce it to its flowering sites as soon as these are vacant, or, if it is to follow some early-spring incident, bring it into the border in late spring.

While on this theme of deliberately and extensively running a bedding plant through other plantings, our favourite for this

▲ *I always grow some of the prostrate pimpernel,* Anagallis monellii *subsp.* linifolia, *with intensely blue flowers. Here it makes an apron for dwarf marigold 'Suzie Wong' on the corner of a border, where the self-sowing poached egg plant,* Limnanthes douglasii, *flowers in May (see page 116). The name of the marigold is irresistible and the plant is not bad either. Since seed germinates within a few days, we often sow as late as May to achieve this effect. As soon as Suzie has been rooted out, in November, limnanthes seedlings appear.*

▶▶ *If not a marriage made in heaven, the couple here look well together until the purple orach,* Atriplex hortensis var. rubra, *has to leave the scene. It must be removed before running to seed or you will be plagued with thousands of self-sown seedlings in following years. The tall annual rudbeckia,* R. hirta *'Indian Summer' (1.2m/ 4ft), is one of the best, with large, black centres to the flowers and powerfully yellow rays. It gets going in July and never lets up until the end.*

This fairly heavily shaded corner works hard in every season, starting with snow-drops and culminating with bedding that takes us into autumn.

▲ **In January** the ever-green ferns, Polystichum setiferum Acutilobum Group, which start their new cycle of growth in March, have been cut back a little prematurely at the turn of the year to allow light for the giant snow-drop, Galanthus 'Washfield Colesbourne', to develop. This snowdrop does not produce seed but clumps up rapidly so that it is easy to build up stock. The plain-leaved harts-tongue fern, Asplenium scolopendrium, is enjoying the limy old mortar along the bottom of the wall. Tulips and the rosette-forming spurge, Euphorbia × martini, behind, will take over from the snowdrops in April–May.

▶▲ **By the end of May** Polystichum setiferum Acutilobum Group is back again and the snowdrops are dormant. There are self-sown Welsh poppies, which we prevent from becoming over-prolific by snapping off all their top growth as soon as the first flush is passed. They break off cleanly at ground level, leaving the roots intact. Campanula patula is in flower. This is best treated as a biennial: we sow seed, which we buy, in late August, prick out seedlings into plug trays and pot them on before the winter. They are overwintered in a cold frame and planted out in April in their flowering sites. The plants are dis-carded in late June – long before the seeds ripen – which is why we buy them in.

purpose is *Ageratum houstonianum* 'Blue Horizon'. Mauve, of course, but Mauve Horizon or even Lilac Horizon would sound silly. This makes a decent, not a squat and malevolent (as are so many modern ageratums) plant, perhaps 60cm/2ft tall by the end of the season. It shows up well at a distance. From a retail source, a packet contains far too little seed. Best to go to a wholesaler.

HIT AND MISS

Timing can be tricky with biennial mulleins – *Verbascum*. They need to be sown in late summer or autumn but not so early as to behave as annuals, leaving little or no flower power for the next June, when you need them. We line the seedlings out, having sown them in pots, and those with a yen to flower prematurely will be discarded, the rest planted into their flowering positions in October, most likely, to get established before winter. On heavy soils there is then the problem of water lodging in their woolly rosette crowns and rotting them. You may risk this, or you may, if keen, suspend a pane of glass a couple of feet, horizontally, above each mullein crown, with vertical wire staples hooked over the glass on its four corners. In this way the crowns are kept dry but there is good air circulation. This performance is only necessary with the woolliest-leaved kinds. 'Banana Custard' and 'Snow Maiden' are two seed strains that we have lately taken a fancy to. Well grown, they should flower at 2m/6ft.

Cosmos is something of an enigma. Unfortunately our climate, with insufficiently hot summers, does not suit the exciting orange-yellow *C. sulphureus*, although it is a splendid autumn performer in New England, whose winters are much colder than ours but the

▶▲**In August** *the ferns are interplanted, as is the whole of the border, with a trickle of* Ageratum *'Blue Horizon', grown from seed. As there is very little seed in a packet, we buy in quantity from a wholesaler. It is the only ageratum currently available whose height has not been drastically reduced by breeders with a fixation on dwarf plants. It will bear blue-mauve flowers into October, with the minimum of dead-heading.*

▶▶ *We plant* Cosmos bipinnatus *'Sonata Pink' to succeed the pure white, early-flowering* Allium neapolitanum *with its trickle of dazzling orange Siberian wallflower (see pages 82–3). Here, in August, the cosmos is seen with long-lasting* Allium cristophii *seed heads. In a mixed border we want the bedding plants to gel with their surroundings and achieve this by encouraging a thread or two to extend into and among neighbours. The pointed, glaucous leaves mingling with the cosmos in the foreground belong to* Canna *'Erebus'.*

summers are a lot hotter, which is what this cosmos loves and it will self-sow. I have seen such seedlings rising to 2m/6ft and more. *C. bipinnatus* and its many cultivars are the ones we grow. Here we are up against the day-length problem. Cosmos are naturally short-day plants, which is to say they need comparatively long nights of some twelve hours in order to make flower buds rather than just foliage, as they tend to in our high-latitude summers, when nights are so short.

But the main commercial seed-producing country is Kenya, where nights are around twelve hours year-round. What flowers (and seeds) freely there may fail to flower altogether with us until October, when the nights lengthen, but that's useless to the gardener wanting a long display of at least three months.

I recently bought seed of *Cosmos bipinnatus* 'Dazzler' (an excellent magenta) which were entirely green, making vast plants 2m/6ft tall but never a flower till October. This experience must puzzle and disappoint many gardeners. My own partial solution is to save my own seed from those plants which flowered earliest, hoping that they will produce early-flowering progeny, which they largely do, but if the summer is wet and miserable, they won't ripen seed at all, and I'm thrown on the mercy of a commercial source.

The tall white 'Purity' is as bad as any. Our friend, currently, is the Sonata Series, 'Sonata Pink' and 'Sonata White'. They have grown no more than 50cm/20in tall by the end of the season and all have flowered well and over a long period.

Nasturtiums, *Tropaeolum majus*, are as popular as ever they were and never prettier than when making a curtain of colour against a north-facing fence. But are they wayward? I'll say.

▲ ▲ *May-flowering poached egg plant,* Limnanthes douglasii, *self-sows among clumps of a blue, bulbous Dutch iris. This iris is ignored in subsequent plantings but remains in situ on the corner of the bed. It has been there since the year dot (don't ask the name) and has never failed to flower.*

▲ *The same corner in summer with a dwarf nasturtium,* Tropaeolum, *and again with our old friend* Tagetes patula *'Suzie Wong'. This is an alternative to the blue pimpernel follow-on planting shown on page 109.*

You never know whether it will be a good nasturtium year or not. They can be decimated both by black aphids and by cabbage white caterpillars. If you spray against these, you'll probably find that the plant itself objects to the spray. Best to pick off the pests by hand. If in too rich soil, the flowers will be hidden underneath the foliage, these troubles becoming worse as the season goes on.

But there is a whole range to choose from, some compact, some with the normal urge to climb. They will self-sow freely and, as the years pass by, will increasingly tend to revert to the original nasturtium red colouring. But that's fine by me. It is such a clean colour and looks a treat trailing over a mauve aster, especially August–September-flowering *Aster sedifolius*.

I used to grow the Gleam Hybrids, which are semi-double, yellow and modestly trailing. I shall probably go back to them. Meantime we do enjoy the trailing, variegated-leaved 'Jewel of Africa', which we plant in an old brick cattle-drinking tank that stands about 1m/ 3ft above the ground. We have grown several of the dwarf, bushy, non-climbing kinds and still have the dark-leaved 'Empress of India', which has red flowers. That sows itself pretty true to type.

FRONT-OF-BORDER INHABITANTS

Begonia is an amazing genus with a huge repertoire, both for foliage and for flowers. Fergus and I dote on them, but we do not like the highly dwarfened, dumpy *B. semperflorens*-type, fibrous-rooted kinds that the breeders delight in. However, a begonia trial at Wisley revealed that some of these develop a bit of height and personality, notably 'Stara White' and 'Stara Pink'. Some can be had as plantlets and they quickly grow on. Dragon Wing Red ('Bepared'), a Semperflorens type, is one of these, growing 30cm/1ft or more high and with a long flowering season, excellent for bedding in a shady position. All begonias like a bit of shade, so they make a good understorey and infillers around taller sun-lovers.

Tuberous-rooted begonias can be stored, dormant, under a greenhouse bench or in a cellar for the winter. In early spring you bring them out and start them into growth in damp peat and under close, humid conditions. We have only cold frame protection in which to do this, so they are not started all that early, but it works. Cascading kinds also make good bedders and we like the single-flowered Illumination Series.

Begonias grown for their foliage never become dormant and are kept going on a greenhouse bench until it is safe to plant them out. 'Little Brother Montgomery' is a great favourite, with

▲ Begonias make excellent summer bedding displays in borders that offer light, overhead shade. The dwarf Semperflorens-type 'Stara White' and 'Stara Pink' in flower at the front have bright, fleshy leaves. B. scharffii has bronzed, felted leaves and stems, with flesh pink blossom as a bonus. Through them all we have threaded free-and-easy Ageratum 'Blue Horizon'.

▶ Fibrous-rooted Begonia Dragon Wing Red is very decorative, with pure red flowers and light-reflecting leaves that show up well in shady borders. Behind is the tender fern, Poly-podium aureum, with deeply cut, glaucous fronds, which is taking a breather from winter and spring spent in my dining room.

This succession planting spans eight months: first there are tulips (right), then an early-summer scheme of, say, Osteospermum hyoseroides 'Gaiety Orange' with Heliophila longifolia, followed by the summer high point (above).

▶ Tulipa 'Yellow Emperor', often in bloom before the end of March, is here opening wide in April sun above a carpet of Arabis alpina subsp. caucasica 'Schneehaube' (Snowcap), which flowers into May.

▲ Salvia coccinea 'Lady in Red' and purple Verbena rigida, both grown from seed, are bedded out in July. Flowering here in September, this planting takes us well into October. The bed is in a sheltered spot and behind is a permanent semi-hardy shrub, Eupatorium ligustrinum, growing to 3m/9ft with glossy leaves and a succession of white flower heads from August to November.

beautifully patterned foliage. We take cuttings when we want to increase our stock and there are specialized methods of propagation, which anyone interested should read up.

What shall I say of petunias? I grow hardly any and yet I freely admit that they have a lot going for them, especially in a fine summer. They hate heavy rain (the doubles in particular) and sometimes never recover from it. The red shades are the most susceptible to adverse weather conditions. 'Purple Wave' and, to a lesser extent, 'Lavender Wave' are the two that I regularly grow, because they have a low, ground-hugging habit and are ideal with autumn-flowering colchicums. The flowers of these can rise above the petunias and are not engulfed. But their season is short, whereas the petunias are making a show both before and after the colchicums' appearance.

Although it is seldom advertised as a virtue, I find the scent of petunias, especially the white and blue shades and especially in the evening and night, delicious, although the plants themselves emit a rather sour smell after rain.

The first time I was in Hungary, quite a few years ago, I was struck by the fact that, being in communist Eastern Europe and cut off, till the wall came down, from breeding developments in the West, old, 'unimproved' seed strains of many annuals were still current. The petunias appealed to me, their small flowers being no disadvantage in my eyes, and the strength of their night scent was unbelievable. I brought seed home and continued the line for many years until, one particularly dreary summer, I got no seed at all, and that was that.

SALVIAS AND AMARANTHUS

The best-known bedding *Salvia* is *S. splendens*, wherein not only the flower's corolla but its calyx also is scarlet. Gertrude Jekyll grew it in the red section of her famous colour-graded mixed border, but we may be sure that it was a far more relaxed plant then, before the breeders had dwarfened and densified it, than it is now. However, in a trial of this species at Wisley I noted a taller and more dignified cultivar called 'Rambo'. We grew it in my Long Border behind a swathe of the white, August-flowering *Allium tuberosum* and liked the result. Also scarlet, but smaller-flowered and making a too-rangy plant, is *S. coccinea*, although in this case it has been improved by the breeders' attentions, and the FI 'Lady in Red' as well as the similar (except that its calyx is dark) 'Forest Fire' are very agreeable front-of-border inhabitants. They

▲ Violent pinky-mauve Salvia involucrata 'Bethellii' is a tuberous-rooted perennial sage that cannot be relied upon to come through the winter; to be sure of having plants for bedding out the following summer, we take cuttings to overwinter under glass. Here it is daringly combined with the Collerette dahlia 'Chimborazo' – deep crimson-red 'petals' and a contrasting pale yellow collar flecked red – which is named after an ancient volcano in Ecuador. This partnership may not be to everyone's taste, but I like my bedding to be full of buzz.

▶ ▲ The familiar love-lies-bleeding, Amaranthus caudatus, has tassels that hang vertically to the ground, but there are cultivars that display themselves in a more becoming fashion and do not grovel. A. 'Hopi Red Dye' is an elegant hybrid with well-displayed bunches of red tails, the entire plant being suffused deep reddish-purple. Here it has a curtain of Clematis 'Royal Velours' of similar rich colouring behind and a lighter backdrop of Hedychium densiflorum.

▶ Amaranthus 'Red Fox' is another annual amaranth with an elegant habit. Here, in early September, it is providing intriguing contrast to greeny-yellow Patrinia scabiosifolia, a short-lived but long-flowering perennial which we raise from seed, and Crocosmia 'Late Lucifer'.

contrast well with the foliage of blue lyme grass, *Leymus arenarius*.

At 1.5m/5ft or even more, we have *Salvia involucrata*, of which the best-known variety is 'Bethellii'. It is perennial and will often survive the winter. Its colouring is shocking pink; that is, bright pink with a dash of mauve in it. I can find uses for that and rather fancy it with the apricot-orange dahlia 'David Howard'.

Salvia guaranitica 'Blue Enigma' is true, rich blue, about 1.2m/4ft tall. One must have it. It has tuberous roots like a dahlia's and it is safest to lift some of these in the autumn and overwinter frost-free, taking cuttings from the young shoots in spring. However, of recent years it has survived the winters outside, so one might as well give it the chance. That is good with 'David Howard' dahlias, in a more conventional colour contrast.

Amaranthus is a rather poetic sort of name, coming from a Greek word meaning unfading, since the flower heads retain their colour for a long time. Tennyson's Lotos Eaters were 'Propt on beds of amaranth and moly'. Moly was a fabulous herb, having a white flower and a black root and endowed with magic properties. It was later applied by Theophrastus and others to *Allium moly*, which many of us grow for its cheerful yellow flowers in June. However, its garlic smell is extremely pungent, so the Lotos Eaters can hardly have been polite company, unless you ate it with them (which, no doubt, you would).

The 1m/3ft *Amaranthus hypochondriacus* (another provocative name) and the slightly dwarfer 'Red Fox' have upright flower head 'tails', but the main point of the plants is those forms that are deeply suffused throughout with crimson red. They are hardy annuals and a pleasing change from the better-known love-lies-bleeding (*A. caudatus*), though that is fun, too.

This succession is in an area where a permanent planting of irises and poppies is overlaid with summer bedding that lasts well into autumn.

▲ *A combination I have always enjoyed is the contrast of orange and purple, which you can get in early summer from the unimproved Oriental poppy,* Papaver orientale, *and Siberian irises,* Iris sibirica. *It is easy to have too much of this iris in the border because its spread becomes quite gluttonous after flowering. So the size of a patch should take this into account and only a small piece allowed, the rest being chopped away. The poppy is more easily managed as it can be cut completely to the ground after flowering and interplanted.*

▶ *The intruder, planted in the gaps between the poppies, can be varied from year to year. In this case it is* Dahlia 'Bishop of Llandaff' *which, if punctiliously deadheaded, has a long summer season. Its particular attraction is the quite heavily cut leaves, almost fernlike and deep purple, as a background to pure red flowers. Among and behind it is* Salvia guaranitica 'Blue Enigma'. *This may come through the winter unharmed, but it is safer to overwinter some tubers as you would dahlias. The shrub behind with glaucous, evergreen foliage is* Atriplex halimus.

DAHLIAS

Summer's full glory is epitomized by the lush tender perennials, of which dahlias are the best known. By some, they are reviled as being common and vulgar (two words for the same thing), but they have a great following and deservedly so. We revel in them at Dixter. As regards varieties to grow, you will have your own favourites, but I give a few of mine at the end of this chapter.

Dahlias have been prized as exhibition flowers for monocultures since they came on the scene in the mid-nineteenth century. This use for them has waned and been replaced by dahlias as mixed border flowers. The idea that they need special treatment has proved false. They can hold their own with all sorts of other plants.

Winter has always been a problem; even more so now, perhaps, that many of the most desirable varieties refuse to make decent, fleshy tubers that will carry them through the dormant months without drying out and shrivelling. The professionals grow stock plants as pot tubers. If confined to a small pot, they are far better inclined, than usual, to make decent tubers, which can easily be carried through the winter, but they have to be grown off the scene as they will be unable to make a garden display. In spring these pot tubers will make young shoots that can easily be rooted as cuttings. At Dixter we box the plants up (having cut them down) in old wine crates and the like, working old potting soil in among the roots, which are quite closely set, in an upright position. They are watered heavily and then stored in a dark, cool but frost-free cellar. You can turn your car out of its garage and use that for storage, but ensure that it does not get too cold. They are watered every week or two through the winter months.

In spring they are brought out – not till April here, as we cannot spare our heated glass for this purpose, so they go into a closed cold frame with solid walls, to retain warmth. Sun heat gets them going and at night the glass is covered with protective matting. When they are sprouting well, we harden them off and eventually plant them out. If we want to increase our stock, we take cuttings from the young shoots, which are ideal material when 10cm/4in long, severing them from the stock where the base of the stem just begins to swell above the tuber. A sharp cut with a razor blade is all the preparation the cutting needs. Several are rooted together in each pot and go on from there. We plant out in early July, or a little earlier, but nights should be warm.

Dahlias are generally staked at the time of planting out. We use a stout bamboo cane for each single-stemmed plant. It looks

▲ *'Hillcrest Royal' is
a spiky Medium Cactus
dahlia of rich reddish-
purple colouring. (The blue
element in its red flowers
is invariably lost in colour
printing.) Here, at the top
of the Long Border, in early
October, it shares the lime-
light with one of the most
important fixtures in this
area,* Anemone × hybrida
*'Honorine Jobert', which
has been flowering since
early July. The perennial
sunflower,* Helianthus
*'Lemon Queen', starts
flowering in September.
At the back of the border
the cardoon,* Cynara
cardunculus, *has seed
heads that remain as
features throughout the
winter, sometimes with
caps of snow.*

▶▲ *Canna glauca, with
narrow, bluish foliage and
small, yellow flowers, is
integrated in our Long
Border in the area where
Weigela 'Florida Variegata'
does its anchoring job and
Ipomoea (syn. Mina)
lobata smothers the spent
delphiniums.*

▶ *Canna indica 'Purpurea',
with purple leaves and small
but endearing orange-red
flowers, is one of my most
vigorous and prolific cannas,
seen here in late summer
through a screen of* Dahlia
'Bishop of Llandaff' and
Verbena bonariensis. *The
Japanese banana,* Musa
basjoo, *adds a voluptuous
note at the back.*

pretty horrible, till growth has concealed it, so we don't use *new*
bamboo, which is shiny and obtrusive.

THE VOGUE FOR CANNAS

There has been quite a return vogue for cannas lately, partly helped,
I have to boast, by my proselytizing efforts in books and articles.
The first enthusiasm for cannas was in the nineteenth century,
when they were used for tropical bedding schemes. Nowadays we
integrate them in our mixed borders just as we do dahlias.

Their roots are fleshy rhizomes. We overwinter them in a cellar,
boxed up like dahlias, and they are already growing when we bring
them out, in April, and put them in a deep cold frame that can be
kept closed without interfering with their growth. After hardening-
off, we generally plant them straight into their flowering positions
from their boxes, when we are ready to do so, generally in June.
We make a generous planting of the rather basic but vigorous
2m/6ft *Canna indica* 'Purpurea', whose asset is its wealth of
purplish leaves which make a striking feature on the moist (but

not drowned) margins of the horse pond. This has a mud bottom.

Many cannas are grown for their flamboyant flowers. The breeders, as is the way of breeders, are increasing flower power at the expense of height, which they want to be less than 1m/3ft. Tall cannas are currently less fashionable, though I like them a lot myself.

The first canna trial ever was held by the RHS at Wisley in 2003, making a great show in late summer and early autumn. Alas, it coincided with the introduction, on dormant tubers from Holland, of a virulent new virus disease, which quickly made a travesty of all stock on the trial ground, flowers, stems, foliage, the lot. As all commercial stock in western Europe is imported from the Netherlands, the tragedy was complete. Stock for the trial imported from America, especially Longwood Gardens, was disease-free on arrival but was quickly infected. The future is uncertain. We are exercising great vigilance on our stocks at Dixter, eliminating anything that looks in the slightest suspect. But who knows?

▲ Lobelia cardinalis 'Queen Victoria' (1.2m/4ft and requiring support to halfway up its stems) likes plenty of moisture in summer. It makes basal rosettes of foliage where-with to overwinter; we box these up in soil and protect them in a cold frame, splitting and replanting them the following spring. It is planted here in front of the luminous Canna 'Striata', which holds its leaves, boldly striped green and yellow, more or less upright and flatteringly transfuses backlighting.

We grow cannas in our exotic garden but also, extensively, in the Long Border, their bold foliage being such an asset. A favourite is *C. × ehemanii*, which is distinct from the rest. Its broad, green leaves have a very narrow, purple margin. The inflorescence is not held upright, as in all the others, but arches over and bears flowers in a beautiful shade of pink.

The cannas derived from the moisture-loving *C. glauca* were developed at Longwood Gardens in the USA and embrace a range of colours, though *C. glauca* itself has narrow, glaucous (bluish)

foliage and small but prolific, clear yellow flowers. The main characteristic of the whole group is that they can be grown actually in shallow water, so they make a handsome feature in a pond, where we plunge the entire pot. The salmon-pink 'Erebus' is showy and prolific. Normal border conditions are also perfectly acceptable.

OTHER CONTESTANTS

Some of the herbaceous American *Lobelia* are good value. Not dependably hardy, so we overwinter them in a cold frame, split the old clumps in spring and then bed out. They grow to 1m/3ft or more and like plenty of moisture. One of the oldest, which we still grow, is *L. cardinalis* 'Queen Victoria', with reddish-purple stems and leaves and long spikes of rich red flowers. Each crown throws up one stem, so it is a leggy plant and needs support – one cane at the back and a single tie around each stem. It is terrific in front of a well-variegated strain of the grass *Arundo donax* var. *versicolor*.

The *Lobelia* F1 Fan Series are an improvement, because they branch and make a long-flowering, bushy group. They are green-leaved. The crimson-red strain is, in my opinion, too dark to show up well at a distance. Although slightly variable, Fan Scarlet (correctly 'Fan Scharlach') is the most effective in the Series.

The genus *Hedychium*, hailing from Asia, is related to edible ginger. *H. gardnerianum*, with strongly scented, yellow flowers, blooms too late to be a useful garden plant, except in Cornwall, but has run riot in parts of the North Island of New Zealand, where it is considered a dangerous weed, ousting weaker native flora. The hardiest species in Britain is *H. densiflorum*, with small, biscuit-coloured flower spikes. Much more telling is Kingdon-Ward's introduction, *H. d.* 'Assam Orange', 1.4m/4½ft, with richly coloured flowers. That is hardy and several others are borderline. *H. d.* 'Stephen' was introduced by Tony Schilling and named after his son. Tony also introduced and named *H. coccineum* 'Tara' (his daughter), quite a bold plant with yellow flowers and red stamens. With us it is hardy only in a warm, protected bed (I like that sort of place myself).

All hedychiums have a rhizomatous habit, their fleshy rhizomes right at the soil's surface. The rhizome makes an easily identified new joint annually, the old ones behind the growth tip becoming dormant. If you lift the whole lot, in spring, you can cut the rhizome up at clearly visible joints, rub the cut surfaces with a fungicidal powder, and place in damp peat under close, steamy conditions (I do this in a double cold frame), and they will come

out of their beauty-sleep, so that, during the summer, they can be potted and treated individually.

Streptocarpus are not generally thought of as being suitable for outside bedding in this country. I got the idea from seeing them so treated in Australia, and thought I should have a go. I chose one of the smaller-flowered varieties, the blue 'Constant Nymph'. It was planted out in part shade when the nights had warmed up, as streptocarpus cannot stand the blaze of midsummer sunshine. They take quite a while to settle down. I ran them through other shade lovers, ferns and low begonias. The streptocarpus really come into their own in September. This is fun gardening.

So is *Farfugium japonicum*, an evergreen perennial. I first saw it in Japan in October. It is a Composite and was giving away this fact by flowering with rather common-looking, yellow daisies. I have never seen it flowering in Britain, as our summers are not hot enough to bring it to this state before winter's arrival. Most beautiful, in my opinion, is *F. j.* var. *giganteum*, with rich green, orbicular leaves rising to no more than 30cm/1ft from the ground. Alas, it is extremely slow to increase and is seldom on the market. But it has a number of cultivars, most of them lending themselves to division. I grow three of these, of which the least distinguished (I think) is 'Crispatum', with puckered foliage. My favourite is 'Aureomaculatum'. In this the leaf is generously spotted (large spots) with yellow. The spots are faint on first arriving (and their arrival is spread over a long period), but gradually intensify and brighten. It is a joyful-looking plant, although often ridiculed, the tired but constantly repeated joke being to declare it must have been sprayed with herbicide. There are more enlightened folk who see it as Fergus and I do.

The other variegated cultivar that we grow is 'Argenteum', whose leaves are heavily splashed with white. We have a plant of this which we leave to overwinter outside, placing a plastic-sheeted box over it in hard weather. Most of our stock is lifted in the autumn and overwintered under frost-free glass.

ORNAMENTAL GRASSES

There are some brilliant, although not hardy, grasses that demand our attention. I mentioned *Arundo donax* var. *versicolor* as making a good background for the tall red *Lobelia cardinalis* 'Queen Victoria', but that you must have the best variegation with the broadest white striping. Because of there being so little green, these strains are not as easily propagated as those having more

◀ Mid October and the show goes on. Here, in moist, rich soil with a yew hedge casting just the right degree of shade, are two forms of Farfugium japon-icum: *white-splashed 'Argenteum' at the back with* Begonia scharffii *and yellow-spotted 'Aureo-maculatum' in front. The glossy fern on the left is* Cyrtomium falcatum, *a handsome evergreen which we overwinter indoors.*

◀ ▼ Arundo donax *var.* versicolor *is one of the most beautiful of all varie-gated plants and it stands out well in plantings of ten-der and warm-temperate plants, such as* Lobelia cardinalis *'Queen Victoria', cannas and dahlias. Here it contributes to strongly contrasting colours and shapes, highlighting the lobelia's dark foliage.*

▼ The narrow, reddish-purple leaves and long, coppery tails of Penni-setum setaceum *'Rubrum' are even more emphatic for having the broad, paddle-shaped foliage of* Canna *'Striata' behind. This is mid August and the partnership will persist until we lift the fountain grass in October for overwintering under well-heated glass.*

green but less impact. Nurserymen will be tempted to propagate from the latter. Best to do your own propagating, once you have a good strain. If in late summer you lay stems to float on water, say a water tank or a pond that doesn't freeze, they will make roots at each node and, in spring, you can cut the stem up so as to have a rooted node on each piece and treat them as separate plants.

Old plants that were bedded out may survive the winter, but will be far too slow to return to active growth in spring, so we lift all our stock and overwinter it under glass, dividing it (if it lends itself to any division) when growing again in spring. It is a truly beautiful grass and worth taking trouble over.

A grass that always arouses envy is *Pennisetum setaceum* 'Rubrum', most often seen as a pot plant but an excellent focal point when planted out for the summer. The whole plant, 60cm/2ft high or more, is suffused with reddish purple. The long 'tails', which comprise the flower head, arch over under their own weight. They are riveting. But it is a bit of a swine to look after. The plant needs lifting in autumn, disturbing its roots as little as possible; pot it up and overwinter under well-heated glass. In spring we

split and repot, eventually hardening off to plant out.

Another grass we love but that causes us pangs of anxiety is *Setaria palmifolia*. This is grown entirely for its foliage, which is broad, as grasses go, and bright green. The surface is rough to touch and conspicuously ribbed. A great focal plant, 60cm/2ft tall if it doesn't run up to flower (one hopes it won't and it doesn't always). Again it is tricky to overwinter and again we lift and pot some stock (it is bulky), with as little disturbance as possible. We overwinter under cool but frost-free glass. At winter's end our plants will look a wreck, but there will be signs of life if looked for, and we rescue what we can, potting individual pieces. Gradually life will return to them and we choose warm weather to plant

them out, or else keep them in pots to use as stopgaps later in the summer.

Once setaria gets going, its growth is incredible and we have to remember to leave plenty of space around it. Certainly an exciting plant; one that goes through several phases.

I am trying to titillate you with tricksy plants that are irresistible and must be made a success of. The Egyptian papyrus, *Cyperus papyrus*, is another, with its tall (2.5m/8ft) scapes, crowned by a mop-like sphere of thread-fine foliage. A wonderful foil in an exotic garden for the leaves of a banana. It is easily raised from seed and young plants present no problem, but to save old ones is the devil. We give them our warmest greenhouse, without expecting a lot to have remained alive at winter's end. From seed, this papyrus is easy and seedlings are no problem to overwinter.

STOUT EXOTICS

I shall move on to stouter ingredients for summer planting in the exotic garden. Cordylines – these are generally cultivars of *Cordyline australis* – have many of them demonstrated surprising hardiness, of recent years, thanks to no great winter testing. There has been a cordyline trial at Wisley, and pretty dim they looked *en masse*, in my opinion, but they are valuable solo incidents in mixed plantings. Their narrow, spiky leaves radiate from a central woody stem. The pink, green and cream-variegated *C. a.* 'Torbay Dazzler' is a feast in itself. We grow a few at Dixter and they are useful.

Agaves are good, solid plants, though they don't like their fleshy leaves to be trodden on. They rather resemble yuccas. *A. americana* has sulky bluish-green leaves and a colony looks splendid above a pale gravel sweep. Beth Chatto plunges the odd plant into her gravel garden, in summer, to be a foil to a background of soft, small-leaved plants. I especially like *A. a.* 'Variegata', with cream and green longitudinal bands. If your border needs a definite end-stop, this is ideal. Not hardy, of course, unless you live by the sea.

Beschorneria yuccoides is not unlike an agave or a yucca, with rosettes of glaucous leaves. If growing well, it will, as early as May, throw up (2m/6ft or so) a wildly exciting inflorescence wherein pink is the dominant colour, but combined with green and blue. The display is over rather too early for convenience. Again, hardy by the sea but needing exceptional shelter inland.

Still with yucca-like habit and leaves, but quite soft and flexible, is *Furcraea longaeva*. When it flowers, it dies, but leaves

◀ Cyperus papyrus has a splendid presence with green mops held above the naked stems that ancient Egyptians flattened and dried to make a form of paper. We overwinter it under the warmest glass we can spare, in a pot sitting in a shallow pan of water. We split it in the spring and pot it up for planting out in June. It is easily raised from seed, but seedlings make no show until they are two years old. Papyrus is a wonderful feathery foil to the solid leaves of bananas and cannas, here C. indica 'Purpurea' and, in the fore-ground, C. 'Erebus'. The seedling Eucalyptus gunnii remains in situ through the winter; we grow it for the shape and metallic colouring of its juvenile foliage and cut it hard back in spring to prevent the long, willow-like adult leaves from developing.

▲ Banana sails flap in the background and the huge leaves of Tetrapanax papyrifer beckon at the front, but Furcraea longaeva is the focal point of this tapestry of foliage shapes and colours. It has to be repotted and housed every winter, the rosette of flexible sword leaves grow-ing larger each year. We had one that flowered, which you can see in its pot in the Sunk Garden on page 39, and then died just in time to stop Fergus from killing himself in the effort of overwintering it.

behind hundreds of viviparous offspring, tiny enough for me to bring one home from West Hill Nurseries, near San Francisco. I had it for about seven years, during which it kept getting larger and more imposing but, not being hardy (except on the coast), it had to be lifted every autumn, potted and housed frost-free. This became a mammoth task when it grew large and I told Fergus that it would beat him. It didn't, but he needed help in handling the beast towards the end.

Then, one February, it showed by an elongating crown that it intended to flower. We kept it in its pot this time, and stood it on the floor of the Sunk Garden. It was an amazing sight, that summer. There were small flowers on its 2.5m/8ft inflorescence, and a few of them ripened seed, but more significant were the vegetative babies that were produced. We treated many of them separately and gave others away. Yet others were wasted, I fear. Then, like Tosca and many another operatic heroine, furcraea died and we started all over again. Whew! What a drama!

▲ *Amaranthus hypochondriacus* cultivars
Amaranth
Height: 1m/3ft
Spread: 30–45cm/1ft–18in
Hardy annual, sun
'Hopi Red Dye' and the slightly dwarfer 'Red Fox' have upright flower head 'tails' and are deeply suffused throughout with crimson red. We sow seed in April, under glass, plant out in summer and enjoy the velvet plumes over a long season.

Arundo donax var. *versicolor*
Variegated giant reed
Height: 2m/6ft
Spread: 1.5m/5ft
Tender, sun
Buy or propagate from plants with a broad, white longitudinal stripe either side of a green centre. With us it will survive most winters, but will be slow to get going next season. Better to lift with minimum root disturbance in November, pot up and overwinter under barely frost-free glass.

▲ *Canna* 'General Eisenhower'
Indian shot
Height: 2m/6ft
Spread: 60cm/2ft
Tender, full sun
This canna has broad, bronze leaves which take on beautiful curves, like a piece of sculpture, and are crowned by large, intense red flowers, which remain in good nick into October. Its vigour is only moderate, which can be an advantage. 'Wyoming', slightly taller at 2.25m/7ft, has the best orange flowers. After the top growth has been frosted, cut the plants down, lift the rhizomes and store in old potting soil in a cool but frost-free place. Visit them fortnightly and give them a thorough watering if the soil has nearly dried out.

▼ *Dahlia* 'David Howard'
Height: 2m/6ft
Spread: 45cm/18in
Tender, full sun
A small, apricot-orange

Decorative, this is deservedly one of the most popular dahlias. Above bronze foliage, it carries a prodigal, non-stop succession of blooms that show up brightly from afar. Deadheading is not vital, as far as looks go, as faded blooms are concealed with further upward growth. We plant out tubers in early June, or a little earlier if nights are warm. Good with blue salvias. Protect from slugs.

Dahlia 'Bishop of Llandaff'
Height: 1.2m/4ft
Spread: 45cm/18in
Tender, sun
With semi-single, pure red flowers and purplish leaves that are almost fernlike in their dissection, the Bishop is probably the most popular dahlia of all, though there are many different strains going under its name. It is the only dahlia which garden snobs allow in their borders, the rest of the genus being considered vulgar. There is a growing vogue for singles, one of the most popular being 'Moonfire' (above). Try it and you'll see why.

▶ *Farfugium japonicum*
Height (foliage only): 25cm/10in
Spread: 40cm/16in
Semi-tender, light shade
In Japan the summers are warm enough to coax this into flower, but the yellow daisies do the plant no service. It has a number of cultivars, but none so handsome as the plain, glossy-leaved *F. j.* var. *giganteum* which, unfortunately, is slow to increase. The orbicular leaves, up to 15cm/6in across, deep green and glossy, are as handsome as any. In 'Aureomaculatum' the leaf has large, yellow spots, faint at first but they gradually intensify and brighten. 'Argenteum' is splashed with white. We treat it as bedding, lifting it and keeping it under frost-free glass for the winter. It likes moist, rich soil.

Hedychium densiflorum 'Stephen'
Ginger lily
Height: 1m/3ft
Spread: 45cm/18in
Borderline tender, sun or light shade
It has thickish, short, cream-yellow spikes and a delicious night scent. We lift the fleshy rhizomes in spring, cut them up at clearly visible joints, rub the cut surfaces with a fungicidal powder, and place in damp peat under close, steamy conditions (I do this in a double cold frame). During the summer, they can be potted and treated individually.

▼ _Helianthus_ 'Valentine'
Sunflower
Height: 2m/6ft
Spread: 45cm/18in
Annual sunflowers are generally single-stemmed, often outrageously clumsy and have far too short a season for our purpose. What's needed is a

smaller-flowered cultivar with a branching habit. 'Valentine', with pale yellow flowers and a dark disc, has great staying power and is far and away the best. I grow it every year.

Hunnemannia fumariifolia 'Sunlite'
Mexican tulip poppy
Height: 50cm/20in
Spread: 25cm/10in
Tender, sun
This is perennial, but generally grown as an annual, which on the Wisley trial ground was better when direct-sown than when planted out from containers. The poppy-like flowers are bright, clear yellow and set off by lacy, glaucous foliage. An excellent combination. 'Sunlite' has an extra row of petals to the normal species. In a scorching summer it flowers from July to late October.

Pennisetum setaceum 'Rubrum'
Fountain grass
Height: 60cm/2ft
Spread: 45cm/18in
Tender, sun
Both the leaves and the pendulous 'tails' which comprise the flower head are suffused with reddish purple. Lift the plant in autumn, disturbing its roots as little as possible,

pot up and overwinter under well-heated glass. In spring we split and repot, eventually hardening off to plant out.

Ricinus communis 'Carmencita'
Castor oil plant
Height: 2–3m/6–10ft (as an annual)
Spread: 1m/3ft
Tender, sun
We grow it from seed each year for its lush, palmate, rich reddish-purple foliage and for the prickly, red seed heads which make for added interest.

Setaria palmifolia
Palm grass
Height: 60cm/2ft
Spread: 1m/3ft or more
Borderline hardy, sun or partial shade
Clump-forming, this grass has broad ribbed foliage of a very bright green, the surface rough to touch. A great focal plant, it is worth the effort of lifting and potting some stock to overwinter under cool but frost-free glass.

Streptocarpus 'Constant Nymph'
Cape primrose
Height: 30cm/1ft
Spread: 38cm/15in
Tender, partial shade
The cape primrose makes rosettes of finely hairy leaves. 'Constant Nymph' is a smaller-flowered

variety, the blue flowers having pale yellow throats and deep mauve veins on the lower lobes. We plant it out in part shade with ferns and low begonias when the nights have warmed up, anticipating its full glory in September.

Rudbeckia hirta 'Indian Summer'
Black-eyed Susan
Height: 1m/3ft
Spread: 60cm/2ft
Tender, sun
A really bold annual rudbeckia, which sometimes survives the winter and flowers a second year, this has large, deep yellow flowers and a black disc. It is a mainstay from early July on, sown from seed in spring.

◀ _Tagetes patula_
French marigold
Height: 45cm/18in
Spread: 45cm/18in
Tender annual, sun or partial shade
I saved my own seed of 'Cinnabar', a dwarf bronze single with a very thin, orange rim, over many years, always taking it from the tallest plants, so that I now have what I consider to be a very presentable, tallish strain. 'Striped Marvel' alternates bronze and orange striping that radiates from the centre of a single bloom and grows on a tallish plant.

The charm of
SELF-SOWERS

Self-sowing plants plug gaps with relaxed abandon and are a great help in keeping the show going, as long as you treat them as allies that need to be controlled.

◄ I begin and end this chapter with the back drive down to our kitchen. The retaining walls on either side are full of interest – some of it originally planted, some self-sowing and perpetuating. In April the emphasis among the aubrietas is primroses, sometimes coloured, white honesty or money flower, Lunaria annua, and forget-me-nots, Myosotis. In June there will follow a sheet of white ox-eye or moon daisies, already visible as plants, and seen at their best in the photograph on pages 156–7.

Gardens that give space to self-appointed volunteers have a comfortable, personal feel. A plant ripens seed after flowering; it falls to the ground, germinates in due course (sometimes after a considerable interval) and produces another generation. So far, you have had no control over the situation. This is when many gardeners get frightened, have visions of a garden overrun by thousands of seedlings with nothing much else visible by midsummer. They remove the lot and apply thick mulches to prevent further germination. Control is restored, but what a lot they are missing!

It is true that if you don't watch out, self-sowers can take you over, and if you see a garden overrun with fennel (*Foeniculum vulgare*) you'll know what sort of gardeners own it. A deep-rooting perennial herb, this makes a tall plant, up to 3m/10ft. (It has a very strong flavour and is recommended to eat with fish. I far prefer dill, myself.) Brian Halliwell, when in charge of the bedding-out department at Kew, had the most successful idea of growing purple-leaved fennel, *F. v.* 'Purpureum', from seed and bedding out the seedlings interplanted with pale yellow tulips. Now you too might just as well, from the start, grow this purple-leaved variety. It is more attractive and comes purple from seed. If you cut all but one plant right to the ground before its seeds ripen, thus saving yourself a lot of trouble from self-sowns later, it will refurnish with a low cushion of young foliage at the end of the season.

▲ *Steady as a rock over many years, Euonymus fortunei 'Silver Queen' is one of the most important anchor plants in the Long Border, but minor infiltrations by self-sowers are still welcome. In this case forget-me-nots, which form a self-sown theme right through the border. Where they are deficient we make up their numbers from elsewhere, the best plants often coming from the vegetable garden. The blue of the forget-me-nots* combines well with the immature euonymus foliage whose yellow leaf margins become silver in maturity.

▼ *The accidental quality of self-sowers is one of their greatest charms. In the crutch of a fig tree at the base of a wall a blackbird sowed the seed of Arum italicum* subsp. *italicum 'Marmoratum'. This would never have occurred by design.*

For self-sowers to contribute to our successions, then, we need to think adventurously and to strike a balance. It is not a simple either/or situation – that is you either put your oar in or you don't. We need to examine and pass judgement on the alternatives.

SEVEN GOOD THINGS ABOUT SELF-SOWERS

1   They cover the ground and do a certain amount of gardening for you. *Mysotis* (forget-me-nots) self-sow intensively and, up to the end of May, you are delighted to have them.

2   They throw up interesting combinations that you might not (probably wouldn't) have dreamt up for yourself. Two self-sowers once did this for me in unison and we were so pleased with the result that we photographed it (just as well we did, as it didn't happen again). A pink volunteer *Alstroemeria* flowered with a self-appointed *Lychnis coronaria*, which is the one with magenta disc-flowers above woolly, grey stems and foliage. This lychnis does all sorts of unexpected things, often entirely breaking the rules of good taste. Gardeners who concentrate on colour harmonies are utterly disconcerted. They usually hate to remove any plant that is flowering and making a show, but are disgusted by the actual show made. Usually the show wins. In another instance the lychnis seeded itself bang in front of a group of fiery red *Crocosmia* 'Lucifer'. That put a smile on my face.

3   Self-sowers may form a theme, running through a considerable length or area of border or garden. *Oenothera glazioviana* and opium poppies (*Papaver somniferum*) will do this and so will *Verbena bonariensis*, if your climate allows it to self-sow at all.

4   They appoint themselves to places where you wouldn't have dreamt of planting them. It might be a tall teazel, *Dipsacus fullonum*, or a hollyhock, *Alcea rosea*, at the front of the border. Often they turn up where it wouldn't have been possible to plant anyway, such as in the narrow cracks of a retaining wall or paving. A blackbird sowed *Arum italicum* 'Pictum' (correctly *Arum italicum* subsp. *italicum* 'Marmoratum'), with beautifully pale-veined leaves all winter, in the crutch of a multi-stemmed wall fig. We would never have thought of attempting that.

Eupatorium purpureum makes far too dense a crown to plant anything in it, yet wild violets have seeded themselves on top and get their flowering over before the host has woken up. Violets and primroses behave similarly under deciduous shrubs, getting their business done before the shrubs leaf out.

And there is often a no-man's-land between hedge and lawn, where things will seed, especially *Campanula persicifolia*, which will actually peer out of the hedge bottom itself.

5   Self-sowers add charm to a garden. Their cheek is endearing (but, of course, it mustn't be allowed to go too far, or 'Who's master here?' will echo down the vales).

6   They play a vital role in successions. For instance, under the naked branches of *Clerodendrum bungei*, self-sown Welsh poppies, *Meconopsis cambrica*, take over from earlier snowdrops.

7   They may be useful pointers to future action. If the common male fern turns up, it will be much too humdrum to keep, but it will have suggested to you that this is a suitable site for a more interesting fern with which to replace it. Then, again, if your myosotis, which should be a picture of health, in fact look peaky, you will be led to ask yourself why. They may be overcrowded, but, equally, the soil may need improving. (Unhealthy weeds are a similar warning signal. Make sure your weeds are lush.)

BEWARE THE DOWNSIDE

1   Self-sowers may overpower their neighbours. They need thinning and controlling in good time. Seeding is crazily prolific once *Smyrnium perfoliatum* is established (it takes three years), so we pull out all but a plant or two immediately after flowering.

2   They may need thought and action and are therefore extra work and effort (good for you).

3   They can look messy and chaotic. Up to you, old fellow.

4   You cannot build a garden with self-sowers. They are just one (amusing) layer. Make sure there's stuffing behind them.

5   They can be a positive problem. I am fond of the annual *Impatiens balfourii*, but when I see it has escaped from its allotted stronghold, I get nervous. It is quite aggressive and its spreading habit can easily elbow out precious things. Also, if it is allowed to seed incontinently, for its seeds are flung far and wide, you'll be in trouble.

6   If you have to wait long for seed to ripen, all those browning plants can easily make a whole border look senile.

7   You can, inadvertently, encourage bad forms of self-sowns through not extracting them before thc damage has been done. Astrantias can become a dreadful bore and they revert to an undistinguished anonymity. Furthermore, they quickly develop a tough rootstock (as does *Alchemilla mollis*), which is an effort to deal with efficiently.

▲ *Self-sowers usually have an official, planned partner of a more static disposition, but in this case two of them had the same idea at the same time:* Alstroemeria ligtu *hybrid and* Lychnis coronaria. *One magenta, the other peachy pink, they gave us a delightful surprise, but unfortunately broke up their partnership of their own accord in following years.*

▶▶ *You can plant biennial* Verbascum olympicum *in autumn or depend on self-sowns appearing in different places in different years. By July they have soared to 2.5m/8ft and are part of the Long Border display. The heavy candelabrum of yellow blossom, which lasts for many weeks, may mean that some plants need staking.* Senecio doria *(2m/6ft), however, with* wide platforms of yellow blossom above glossy, dark green leaves, is self-supporting. *The pink phlox, between whose groups are threaded late-flowering tulips, is quite heavily fed and may not need replanting more often than every five years.* Salvia sclarea *var.* turkestaniana *(on the left) is biennial and may be substituted by something different in other years. It finishes flowering by mid July and may be replaced by cannas and dahlias. Shrubby* Hoheria glabrata *looks like cherry blossom but has a short season.* Clematis 'Jackmanii Superba', *trained up a 3m/ 10ft pole, is cut more than half way back each late November, starting up again the following spring.*

Lutyens' bold structure in the Walled Garden has two terminal archways of Moresque design, both framing views of parts of the garden on different levels. Here, looking along a hard-working border by the wall, you become increasingly aware of the developing scenario beyond the arch, with the shingle-tile barn at the far side. The Barn Garden and Sunk Gardens are almost a garden in themselves, so they are a magnet for your approaching footsteps.

The border shown in this series of photographs needs to provide a continuing but ever-changing introduction as you approach the steps, from winter right through to autumn. Self-sowers are a part of the relaxed ambience that is an important message throughout the garden.

◀▲ **January**: the most important self-sowing element in the border is the row of hartstongue ferns at the bottom of a rubbly wall. They like the lime in the mortar and are only fully revealed when other border contents have died down or been removed. Meanwhile Galanthus 'Washfield Colesbourne' is a snowdrop that clumps up quickly. It makes a display at the corners of the beds and beneath the white winter stems of Rubus cockburnianus 'Goldenvale'.

▲ **The second week of May**: essential padding for the tulips, T. 'Spring Green', is here created by forget-me-nots and the acid yellow of Smyrnium perfoliatum.

▶▲ **For May and June**: self-sowing Welsh poppies, Meconopsis cambrica, are deliberately inter-planted with the biennial Campanula patula, *which makes a good contrast.*

▶ *Early October*: the self-sown features here are the teazel, Dipsacus sylvestris, whose skeleton will last the whole winter, and, to the right, a bird-sown Cotoneaster horizontalis on top of the wall, which is bright with berries. The Welsh poppies are perennial and have been cut down. We have replaced them with a ribbon of Ageratum houstonianum *'Blue Horizon'*.

Self-sown aquilegias of the *Aquilegia vulgaris* type are early
in bloom and run to seed amazingly fast. I hate the spurless
Norah Barlow types myself, but they are easily missed, as seed
follows flowers so quickly. Any of this species can easily over-
whelm smaller, slower-to-get-going plants.

Verbascums are incredibly promiscuous. *Verbascum
phlomoides* seems to me greatly inferior to *V. olympicum*, both
of them biennials and not dissimilar in leaf. You need to learn
what you should look for. If you don't want pink foxgloves
among your whites – I write of the biennial *Digitalis purpurea*
types – you should learn to spot the difference while they
are still just leafy young seedlings, those that will be pinkish
having pink-suffused leaf stalks. It's a great game.

Many of the bulbs and spring woodlanders which I described as sharing the same space with perennials spread by self-sowing, among them snowdrops and crocuses, *Scilla bithynica*, small anemones and celandines, followed by species tulips and alliums. Now let's be cheered by primroses in spring since they self-sow almost anywhere, other than in blazing sun. I'm talking of the wild kind, *Primula vulgaris*, which should be obtained in a local strain. It naturalizes easily, especially in shady places, and is an opportunist in most of my borders, putting itself wherever survival seems most likely. As the seeds do not spread far, you can give it a helping hand. On a steep, shady bank, plant several plants from different sources (to ensure cross-pollination) at the top and they will make their way downwards (isn't gravity wonderful?).

Violets extend the season in the same way. They are complex and I do not pretend to be an expert. Scented violets, *Viola odorata*, grow wild in many areas, mostly alkaline. Local colour strains vary a great deal, which can be quite exciting. The edge of woodland is their favourite habitat. They naturalize in my garden to an extent, the white 'Alba' readily extending its range. It turns up in all sorts of welcome places, like paving cracks, and underneath my rather sparsely growing Jerusalem sage, *Phlomis fruticosa*.

I have several strains or species of odourless violets, all of which we dub dog violets. They are common in the woods around me and they seed freely throughout my garden, being great opportunists and using any spot where they will be left to get on with life, undisturbed. March–April is the season for all these violets,

▼ Helleborus foetidus, the so-called stinking hellebore (really quite an agreeable planty smell), is a sub-shrubby, evergreen self-sower whose dark green leaves are pedate, the fingers distributed about an arc. It is a great feature at all times, with no need for flowers to pep it up. It turns up at the margin of my Long Border and is arresting even when most other contents are being winsome and colourful. The flowers, from January onwards, are by no means to be despised, in a complex inflorescence of green, purple-margined bells that last well into spring. I find that plants are best renewed every other year.

though they have a way of throwing up blooms in any month of the year.

When fresh, in spring, *Barbarea vulgaris* 'Variegata' is a charmer which sows itself true without reverting. The type is an entirely undistinguished crucifer that would be dubbed a weed in any situation, but this yellow-variegated cultivar makes dazzling incidents in your borders. You never quite know where it will turn up, but it is never uncomfortably prolific. Its golden foliage over a long season loses its shine when flowering takes over, but you need to leave a few in place to set seed.

Hellebores are among the freest self-sowers and a great support in the early months of the year. The semi-woody *Helleborus foetidus* is a British native of alkaline woodland and an extremely handsome plant. It is not noted for being long-lived and youngish plants give best value. It turns up in odd places of its own choice in my mixed borders and shows up at most times of the year because of its distinctively shaped leaves, with fingered segments, and of its dark, rich green colouring at every season. It flowers from January to April, with generous panicles of pale green flowers margined in purple. There are slight variants which, if kept separate from the rest, retain their individuality through the generations.

Helleborus argutifolius, whose name fluctuates between this and *H. corsicus*, is very similar, though not native. It is a lighter-coloured plant with trifoliate leaves edged with mock prickles; and pale green flowers, larger and opening wider, over the same season as *H. foetidus*. In some gardens it makes huge, showy colonies (excellent with ferns) but has never taken a shine on me.

Winter-flowering plants all tend to have a long season, because of the cool weather holding them back. This is equally the case with the so-called Lenten roses, which used to be classified under *Helleborus orientalis*, but which we now have to call H. × *hybridus*. They are herbaceous perennials with soft and sappy flowering stems which collapse during frosty spells and look thoroughly pathetic, but always right themselves as soon as frost relents. There has been a great deal of breeding work done on this section with many lovely results, including a range of doubles that are not in the least vulgar, as doubles can be. All are capable of self-sowing and, if you have no intention of conducting a deliberate breeding programme of your own, it is still fun to collect and grow on seedlings that have arisen close to particularly admired hellebores within your own garden.

▼ *Looking up the Long Border at the end of April, lime-green* Smyrnium perfoliatum *is making an excellent follow-on to Lenten roses,* Helleborus orientalis *hybrids. It takes up to three years for smyrnium seedlings to flower and they then need vigorous thinning to prevent them taking over entirely. After flowering the plant dies, but once established and self-seeding, you won't lose it, ever!*

POTENTIAL THUGS

When seedlings of any plant appear in their thousands, you need to be ruthless about reducing them – by as much as ninety-nine per cent. If you grow *Smyrnium perfoliatum* as a follow-on to early-flowering hellebores, you can easily see where they are and reduce their numbers.

The green and palest green marbled foliage of *Arum italicum* subsp. *italicum* 'Marmoratum', which appears in autumn and may sustain you through the winter months, needs no encouragement. Birds spread its berries – these precede the leaves – so that you'll have it in many places where it is a competitive nuisance. Furthermore, the variegation may be inferior. Hard frost will clobber it but it will return in spring, dying away in summer. Plants are tenacious and quite difficult to extract without leaving parts behind.

◀ Eryngium giganteum, often known as Miss Willmott's ghost, is taking up space that will later be taken up by perennials, such as Cortaderia selloana 'Pumila'. This eryngium is monocarpic but has a taproot so it does not move well. It should not be allowed to self-sow freely. Cut down all the tired-looking plants in July. The yellow-flowered evening primrose, Oenothera glazioviana, has a similar habit, but flowers right into the forenoon. This is in the Barn Garden and one of the four anchoring Osmanthus delavayi can be seen in the background.

▲ Lunaria annua var. albiflora is extremely vigorous. Long before it flowers, it can be identified as the albino by the pale colouring of its leaves. The species in general is tolerant of quite heavy shade.

▲▶ Lunaria annua 'Variegata' is recessive. On its own all the seedlings will come variegated, but if it is near a dominant Lunaria, there will be very few variegated seedlings. This one with its mauve flower is particularly effective with 'Bleu Aimable' tulips. The jagged foliage of a cardoon is seen in the background.

Honesty, or money flower, *Lunaria annua*, is an extremely freely self-seeding biennial which pops up in my borders and, with some control, makes a great companion to spring bedding. The seedlings quickly become quite tough and laborious to remove, but they are easily thinned when no larger than a pair of conspicuous seed leaves, soon after germination, early in their first year. *L. a.* 'Munstead Purple' is a good, rich reddish purple. 'Alba' is pure white with rather paler-than-normal foliage and a strong constitution.

There are at least two variegated-leaved seed strains of honesty. In one of them, *Lunaria annua* var. *albiflora* 'Alba Variegata', the leaf variegation is zoned and well organized, the flowers white. In the other, my preferred one, *Lunaria annua* 'Variegata', the variegation is disorganized in splashes, the flowers being mauve. It is particularly charming mixed in with the mauve tulip 'Bleu Aimable'. This honesty is recessive. If near a plain-leaved one, all its seedlings in the first generation will come plain-leaved, only showing variegation on a one-in-four ratio in the second generation. However, if kept isolated, which is what I attempt to do, all the progeny will be variegated. My attempts are only partially successful, but I practise a bit of roguing. As soon as the true leaves are large enough to show whether they will be variegated or not, I pull out those with plain leaves. And I also do a bit of spacing out with the variegated seedlings, even though they do not take too kindly to disturbance. It can be done.

▼ *The Welsh poppy,*
Meconopsis cambrica, *can be orange but is more typically yellow. Here it is partnered by* Euphorbia griffithii *'Fireglow'. Both plants are quite aggressive and have to fight it out between them, ourselves as referees. The* Cestrum parqui, *seen top right, will occupy this area within a few weeks (see page 64).*

▶ Atriplex hortensis *var.* rubra *is a crazy self-sower and needs stricter control than Fergus is inclined to give it, but, at 2m/6ft, it does create exciting highlights, especially if as here it has the brilliant yellow background of* Carex elata *'Aurea'. Other conspicuous features are the foliage of* Helianthus salicifolius, Phlox paniculata *and the August-flowering poker,* Kniphofia uvaria *'Nobilis'.*

The monocarpic *Eryngium giganteum* (60cm/2ft) is a general favourite, invariably referred to as Miss Willmott's ghost. Whether because she was a pale and prickly lady (she was not popular) or whether because of the fable (which I heavily doubt) that she scattered seeds of it in other people's gardens without saying she had done so, I do not know. It is a stiff and spiny plant in which the central cone of tiny flowers is surrounded by a handsome silvery ruff of bracts. In the strain collected by Martyn Rix in Turkey, and called 'Silver Ghost' by him, the ruff has narrower, spikier segments. That's even better. *E. giganteum* seeds itself all over your borders, but, unless it has plenty of space in which to develop, makes a poor plant. In that case the overcrowded seedlings may take several years to reach flowering size. So, thin them out. Some seedlings will be seen to have narrow, mottled leaves. These will never develop into good plants as they have contracted a virus disease. Chop through the tap root and they won't bother you again. Old plants run to seed in late July and turn a horrid dirty colour. At that stage you should firmly get rid of all but one or two, left to self-sow.

An annual herb, closely related to spinach, that can take over if not controlled, is *Atriplex hortensis* var. *rubra* (2m/6ft) called orach or red mountain spinach. A few plants of it in this its purple-leaved form look very handsome with golden-leaved shrubs, even as the seed heads are ripening, in late summer. But you should remove the plants (quite heavy work) before the seeds are actually shed. The leaves of young plants look nice in a mixed salad, but their flavour cannot touch that of proper spinach.

To keep control of Welsh poppies, *Meconopsis cambrica*, you need to be on the spot when they are running to seed. Just grab all of the top growth and tug: it will break away clearly from the roots. Generally yellow in the wild but often orange in gardens, these poppies give a scattering of blossom all through the growing season and reach a peak in May. They are an excellent under-storey in shady places: for instance, under hydrangeas. A great nuisance, however, when they seed into plants that are weaker-growing than themselves, like small ferns. On the whole, I wouldn't be without them.

LINKING THEMES

The delightful *Papaver commutatum* 'Ladybird' produces little viable seed and rarely self-sows. Shirley poppies, mostly derived from *P. rhoeas*, the scarlet field poppy, self-sow to an extent, but are not to be depended upon. *Papaver somniferum*, the opium poppy,

however, is an important self-sowing poppy which forms a theme running through my borders. It naturally has a single, mauve flower of no great distinction, but many beautiful and varied strains have been bred which come more or less true from seed. Save your own from the best and broadcast the seeds in areas where you would like to see it flowering in June.

Myosotis sylvatica, the April–May-flowering forget-me-nots, are excellent, if under control, to run as a connecting theme through many of your borders. Often the best plants seem to have put themselves in some out-of-the-way part of the garden, perhaps even among the vegetables, but they can easily be moved to where you want them. Plant them sparsely, because individual plants have a considerable spread, when they get going. And only let them loose where they will do no harm by competing with perennials that will need to take over and must have space themselves.

The situation will fully reveal itself when you come to pull the old myosotis plants out, at the end of May. You will then see to what extent, if any, they have inhibited their neighbours' development. But it is best to anticipate, so that no inhibiting occurs. That said, an interrupted haze of self-sown or popped-in myosotis adds great charm to the spring garden, more so than where they have been regularly bedded out with tulips.

Verbena bonariensis is a great favourite in my Sussex garden and makes a linking theme, in summer and early autumn, through my exotic garden. But it is not popular everywhere and in warmer countries is considered a weed of cultivation. Tall (2m/6ft) and stemmy, its stems are green and perform the function of leaves, the actual leaves being quite tiny. At the tops of these stems are its clusters of light purple flowers. It is a see-through plant that can be allowed at the front of a one-sided border, because it doesn't block the view behind.

The evening primrose, *Oenothera glazioviana*, is a shining example of a plant creating an extraordinary theme. It sows itself at every level of our Sunk Garden and the Barn Garden above it.

CRACK PLANTS

Self-appointed plants can contribute without muscling anything out of the border, so, having touched on the subject of paving cracks, I will take it a bit further. You must, of course, go easy on the herbicides but you must also exercise some control. Otherwise, for instance, your sitting-out area can completely disappear in a mass of herbage. On our terrace I have the brown, yet lively

▲ Verbena bonariensis *has little leaf and exists by nature of its green stems. It is thin textured but, since it needs plenty of light at the base of the plant, thrives best at the front margin of the border. Through it can be seen an old colony of* Alstroemeria ligtu *hybrids, pink phloxes, the fresh green foliage of* Helianthus salicifolius, Senecio doria *and, at the back,* Clematis 'Jackmanii Superba', *trained up a 3m/10ft pole.*

brown, New Zealand sedge, *Carex buchananii*, which grows in 30cm/1ft tufts. I like to have it here and there, but its flowering stems lie on the paving and, unnoticed, self-sow abundantly, unless shorn back betimes (which seldom happens).

Then there is the wand flower, *Dierama pulcherrimum*, also coyly known an angel's fishing rods (ugh!). It flowers in July from arching rods from which dangle its tubular flowers, usually magenta, but there are plenty of colour variants. They sway attractively in the lightest breeze. The plant has a tough rootstock with narrow, evergreen leaves, usually a lot of dead ones among them. You should clean them up every spring, tugging them out from the base rather than cutting them off. It self-sows with abandon, the seedlings quite hard to extract. Well, I've warned you, but it's still a plant worth including, if you have the space. It grows about 1.5m/5ft tall.

Provided your climate is not too severe, the little Mexican daisy, *Erigeron karvinskianus*, whose flowers open white but change to pink with age, will sow itself in every crack available, horizontal or vertical. Sheer or cut the plants back to base in spring and they'll flower non-stop from May to November.

▼ *The cracks in the paving of our sitting-out terrace seem to be a playground for self-sowers. Notable here is our old friend* Verbena bonariensis, *with light purple flower heads, but more surprisingly* Campanula lactiflora, *which has blown in from a bed some 30m/100ft distant where it grows to 2m/6ft and more. In the terrace cracks we pinch out all the campanula's leaders in May (what's known as the 'Chelsea chop'), so that combined with the constriction of its situation it grows no more than 60cm–1m/ 2–3ft tall. There are the arching, magenta-flowered stems of the wand flower,* Dierama pulcherrimum, *in the background. It is an ardent self-sower; control needs to be exercised.*

◄◄ *Red valerian,* Centranthus ruber, *has roots that are destructive to walls, but we allow some all the same. Cut back after its first flowering, it will generally have a second. The little Mexican daisy,* Erigeron karvinskianus, *whose flowers open white and change to pink with age, self-sows in every available crack. We planted the shrubby* Convolvulus cneorum *as an eye-catcher on top of the wall.*

▶ *Moon daisies,* Leucanthemum vulgare, *with* Euphorbia amygdaloides var. robbiae *in the walls on either side of our back drive. This is the May–June sequel to the scene on page 136. Immediately after flowering all the daisy stems are tugged out, leaving the rest of the plant for another year. It is endlessly self-renewing. The spurge remains presentable until August, but then we cut it down, quite low, to make way for the new crop of leafy rosettes.*

Red valerian, *Centranthus ruber*, is another happy inhabitant of horizontal or vertical cracks. It has long, thick roots with great lateral strength and is justly feared in old walls, being forbidden by English Heritage in any of its buildings, even if already ruins. But it is pretty and I do allow some in my garden. It carries panicles of blossom, principally in June. This may be red, white, a rather dirty pink or, in certain localities, notably I noticed in southwest Scotland, a very nice, soft pink. From flowering, it runs to seed in no time and, as it is a great self-sower, you need to be on the spot, to cut the whole plant hard back. After which it will grow and, if the summer is warm, flower a second time.

A number of *Sisyrinchium* species will sow themselves around and some are entirely worthless. They should be weeded out as soon as seen. The one in my terrace paving cracks is *S. angustifolium*, sometimes called blue-eyed grass. It grows wild in both the west of Ireland and across the pond in America. Only 15cm/6in or so tall, it makes upright tufts of narrow leaves (it belongs to the iris family). The blue flowers, not a very bright blue but pretty in quantity, do not open out till midday, which I find interesting.

Ox-eye daisies, *Leucanthemum vulgare*, are surprisingly successful in drystone retaining walls. We have one that is a sheet of them, all self-appointed, and they take over, in early summer, from a spring display with aubrieta, primroses and *Euphorbia amygdaloides* var. *robbiae*. When they are in flower, you'd think that there was nothing but the ox-eyes there. As soon as they have finished, you should grab all their flowered stems in handfuls, low down, and tug. They will break off at the base, leaving the rootstock for another year, but all will be tidy and clean again.

I shall bring in martagon lilies, *Lilium martagon*, because they are welcome self-sowers with me and rather versatile in the way that they will wander about, sometimes appearing in paving cracks where they are harmless but totally unexpected. This is a June-flowering turkscap with, I have to admit, rather muddy purple flowers. There are improved strains, including the scintillating albino, but you cannot expect too much of self-sowers, which have a habit of returning to the type.

In a multi-layered garden self-sowers contribute informality, charm and a certain richness to your official plantings. If you work with them, controlling yet learning from them, they will provide great back-up in your goal of having a garden that always looks positive.

Alcea rosea
Hollyhock
Height: up to 3m/10ft
Spread: 1m/3ft
Hardy, rich well-drained soil, sun
A familiar, tall perennial, the hollyhock is normally consigned to the back of any planting. But if it is a dark, maroon-flowered strain (with white stigma and stamens), you will see it better close-up, so I like to plant some (but they also self-sow) at a border's margin. There should be paving cracks at hand into which they can spread seed. Rust disease is the bane of hollyhock growers. Miss Jekyll was complaining about it in the late nineteenth century, but we are still growing them. Spray before the trouble appears and repeat the treatment a couple of times during the summer.

▲ **Atriplex hortensis var. rubra**
Purple orach
Height: 2m/6ft
Spread: 60cm/2ft
Fertile, moist, but free-draining soil, sun
An annual herb, closely related to spinach, grown for its rich purple foliage and upright habit, as well as its purple-red fox-tail-like flowering spikes in summer. Seedlings often insinuate themselves in unlikely places, such as in a tussock of Bowles's golden sedge (*Carex elata* 'Aurea'). Even as the seed heads are ripening, in late summer, purple orach looks very handsome. But you should remove the plants (quite heavy work) before the seeds are actually shed.

▶ **Campanula lactiflora**
Bellflower
Height: 2m/6ft
Spread: 60cm/2ft
Hardy, sun
A principal mainstay of my early-summer borders and one of the tallest hardy perennial species, this is typically mauve, the flowers making large, domed bells. It self-sows and appoints itself (to my delight) among hydrangeas. I welcome it in paving cracks, too, in which situation you want to pinch out the growing points in May when the plant is about 30cm/1ft high. You can also take cuttings of young shoots, which easily root. After its flowering in July, dead-head it and it often branches from below your cut and produces a small second crop.

▲ **Limnanthes douglasii**
Poached egg plant
Height and spread: 15cm/6in
Hardy annual, sun
A white and yellow annual from California, this self-sows heartily but needs light if it is to germinate. I have it taking turn and turn about on the corner of a border, with marigolds (one I like is 'Suzie Wong' – the name is irresistible). As soon as Suzie has been rooted out, in autumn, limnanthes seedlings appear and overwinter, being hardy. They'll flower in May. A good succession.

Lychnis coronaria
Rose campion
Height: 1m/3ft
Spread: 60cm/2ft
Hardy, sun
A short-lived perennial that seeds freely and will be found infiltrating and livening up all sorts of summer plantings. A long succession of disc-shaped, vivid magenta flowers (but there are gentrified forms of softer colouring) open singly but will not last the summer through, so we pull the plants out in late July or cut them back if still healthy to do a second year.

▼ **Oenothera glazioviana**
Evening primrose
Height: 2m/6ft tall
Spread: 80cm/32in
Hardy, sun
The largest-flowered evening primrose has scented blooms that last all night and well into the next forenoon. With me it sows itself at every level of our Sunk Garden and the Barn Garden above it, creating an extraordinary theme in July.

▶ *Papaver somniferum*
Opium poppy
Height: 1.2m/4ft
Spread: 30cm/1ft
Tender, sun
I have had a double pink opium poppy for as long as I can remember, and it still comes back. Any that are below par I pull out when they reveal themselves. Most of this poppy's seed will germinate in spring and flower in June. But some will germinate in the autumn. These are likely to get killed in the winter but the few which survive will make enormous plants and be quite exciting as specimens, rather than mere units. It works well among other self-sowers, such as *Campanula persicifolia*, *Lychnis coronaria* and foxgloves.

▶ *Persicaria orientalis*
Prince's feather
Height: 3m/10ft
Spread: 60cm/2ft
Hardy annual, sun
This annual is at its peak in September, when most others are failing. The tiny flowers, borne in short, drooping 'tails', retain their rich pink colouring for many weeks and you will be surprised to find, if you pick one and rub

it between the palms of your hands, that ripe, black seeds reside within and are now revealed. Its seedlings are on the tender side and yet, if you sow it under glass, the seeds won't germinate. They need a cold period to break their dormancy. We let it self-sow, which it does freely. The seed germinates *in situ*. We dig up as many seedlings as we need and bring them on under glass, harden them off and plant them as a follow-on to spring bedding.

▲ *Smyrnium perfoliatum*
Perfoliate alexanders
Height: 60cm–1.5m/2–5ft
Spread: 60cm/2ft
Hardy, any soil, sun or partial shade
Monocarpic plant that dies after flowering. It looks like a euphorbia from a distance since foliage, bracts and tiny flower umbels are bright acid-green, in late spring and early summer.

Smyrnium is a bit sneaky. First, you have trouble in establishing it at all, as its seed must be sown fresh and then takes three years to reach flowering size, during which time you may unthinkingly weed it all out. But then, when it does start flowering, its seeding is crazily prolific. Immediately after flowering, we pull out all but a plant or two.

Verbascum olympicum
Biennial mullein
Height: 2.25m/7ft
Spread: 1.2m/4ft
Hardy, sun
The noblest mullein self-sows, often in the most appropriate places. We leave seedlings *in situ* but also move them around to form themes or incidents through a border. In its second year a stout, upright stem branches

into a symmetrical candelabrum of clear yellow blossom, which lasts over a long high-summer season.

▶ *Verbena bonariensis*
Argentinean vervain
Height: 2m/6ft
Spread: 30cm/1ft
Hardy, well-drained soil, sun
This short-lived perennial is a see-through plant that can make a linking theme running through a border, starting in mid-summer and building to a climax in September. Second-year plants, which have survived the winter (if they have), start flowering in late June. The current season's seedlings later take over, flowering in October. All this supposes that your verbenas have managed to set and distribute ripe seed, but in climates

colder than mine they will fail to do so and if you want to perpetuate your own stock you may have to root cuttings and overwinter them under glass.

CLIMBERS
for interest skywards

Climbers are invaluable adjuncts to succession plantings. They intensify the main display and often take over completely from it.

◀ *The annual morning glory, Ipomoea tricolor 'Heavenly Blue', can be popped in in all sorts of unexpected places to clamber over a range of surprised hosts. It is one of the most exciting flowers in the morning garden when the colour is quite an electric blue. This takes on a mauve tinge towards midday and the flower crumples in the afternoon. The seedlings are very temperature-sensitive and will turn yellow if the weather is too chilly for them.*

Whereas most gardeners think of climbers as clothing for walls and trellises, which is essential, to the adventurous-minded, this is a ridiculously limited assessment of their potentialities. Their most obvious use is to add pizzazz to plants that have a magnificent but short season of interest. Take spring-flowering shrubs, for example, and in particular the evergreen rhododendrons which, apart from a blaze of colour for about three weeks, are just dull lumps of heavy foliage for eleven months of the year. A correctly chosen climber (or several of them), planted on the outside of the bush in well-prepared soil, can transform the situation, taking over from the rhodo, maybe in June, when it has finished its display, and continuing through the rest of the summer. Clematis are naturally adapted to growing through other vegetation, so they are often excellent for the job and you'll find a lot of them in this chapter.

Clematis come to the rescue in other ways: for instance, what to do about *Paeonia lactiflora* hybrids when they leave you in the lurch after their flowering with most of summer still ahead? One idea (not mine) that can work well is to interplant them with a *Clematis flammula* or two (or more, according to the size of the peony planting). This seethes with tiny, white, heavily scented flowers shown off by dark green foliage. Its vigour is by no means outrageous and it flowers on its young growth in August, so you can cut it hard back at the end of its season. Don't give it any support; just let it crawl.

▼ In spring a display of 'Yellow Emperor' tulips (below) occupies the area where the extremely vigorous Clematis × jouiniana *'Praecox' takes over in June, July and August (bottom). It has a non-climbing herbaceous clematis,* C. heracleifolia, *as one of its parents, so its growth needs guiding into its neighbours: some is tied to a pole and some strays into and up the bamboo, but most of it grows on the flat, swallowing up the space as it develops. The green columns of* Helianthus salicifolius *give this scene a lift over a long season. The buddleja behind is* B. davidii *'Dartmoor'. The lower picture was taken before the grass was replaced by paving.*

You should also interplant your peonies with hyacinths, for the spring. Their flowers look wonderful with the peonies' crimson young shoots as a foil. Now we have a triumphant succession after all. We might even interplant with large-flowered gladioli. With such a radiant vision for the future, surely not everything can go wrong.

Climbers are a tremendously varied lot and are not just limited to the obvious kinds like clematis, honeysuckles and summer jasmine. They may be herbaceous perennials or they may be annuals. Their uses in promoting our theme of successions will vary accordingly.

UP A POLE, TRIPOD OR WIGWAM

Climbers take up the minimum of lateral space this way and can, so to speak, increase the size of our garden by reaching towards the sky above it. Something for nothing appeals to me. Of course the tripod may be quite low and I don't altogether favour it because your climber or climbers seem never to clothe it fully. A 3m/10ft pole they do, by midsummer anyway.

Poles of various heights have a second important use: that of taking some (possibly most) of the weight off the neighbouring shrub into which you would like to see the climber threading its way. If you have planted a climber next to a host shrub and the former is found to be too bulky for the job, an adjacent pole will solve your problem.

ON THE FLAT

Climbers don't have to climb. My old friend John Treasure, gardening at Burford House in the Teme valley, south Shropshire, was keen on heathers and grew clematis among them. But there were also upright cone-shaped conifers among the heathers, so the clematis were encouraged to stray into and up these.

At Dixter I have a strong old specimen of *Clematis × jouiniana* 'Praecox', which is non-climbing but covers itself from late June on for three months with hosts of small, cruciform, skimmed-milk blue flowers. It is planted at the back of a one-sided border and cut hard to a stump in winter. But some of its growth is tied to a pole at the back. It also strays into and up a nearby bamboo. But the bulk of it grows on the ground and when fully developed spreads forwards on to the paving at the border's front margin. In the meantime we use the still-vacant ground, first with the early-flowering Fosteriana tulip 'Yellow Emperor', then with the annual

▼ Clematis recta 'Purpurea' is generally raised from seed and is therefore a variable product. You should make sure that you get a dark-leaved seedling. It has two seasons. In spring, before it needs any support, it makes a beautiful cushion of rich purple foliage. We put in pea-sticks when growth is about knee high and beginning to arch over, but earlier if rain is forecast.

▲ The peastick palisade allows Clematis recta 'Purpurea' to grow 2–3m/ 6–10ft tall and is just visible still at the end of May, but scarlet Papaver orientale is looking so super in front of it that one hardly notices (one being me, of course!). The support will be dis-guised further by the time the clematis is covered in a foam of tiny cruciform flowers.

Nigella hispanica. Further back, annual *Ammi majus* and single blue larkspur 'Blue Cloud'. These are tallish and will have to be staked, but they finish quite early. Alternatively we may use ladybird poppies, *Papaver commutatum*, sown in autumn or early spring so as to flower early. All these are swept aside as the clematis swallows up the space.

ON PEASTICKS OR BRUSHWOOD

I have the early, large-flowered, blue *Clematis* 'Lasurstern' growing on peasticks in the Long Border. The peasticks need replacing annually, because the old ones become brittle, but that is no great problem if your peasticks are easily obtained – generally from coppiced woodland. Hazel and hornbeam are ideal, in my area. Birch can be good, too.

I also use peasticks to support the herbaceous, climbing perennial pea, *Lathyrus grandiflorus.* It makes a curtain of growth up the sticks so as to reach into the lowest branches of a pollarded willow, *Salix alba* var. *sericea.* The magenta pea (which is quite a traveller by suckering, I may say) contrasts handsomely, in June, with the willow's silvery foliage. Later, when that show is over, cannas or other tender perennials bedded out in front of them will do a masking act.

▼ Delphinium 'Mighty
Atom' is rather later
flowering than the general
run of delphiniums and
not so inconveniently tall.
But once it has finished,
something needs to be
done. We cut the dead
spikes back to where the
leaves begin and plant
several plants of the
annual Ipomoea (syn.
Mina) lobata around it.

▶ In early September
Ipomoea (syn. Mina)
lobata has taken over the
space completely, although
the delphinium remains
healthy in a dormant state.
By now Viburnum opulus
'Compactum' behind it
has reddened its fruit and
Canna 'General Eisenhower'
is about to flower. This
succession can be seen in
the plans on page 29.

ON PERENNIALS

We (Fergus in particular) are keen on the generous use of *Ipomoea lobata*, better known, perhaps, as *Mina lobata*, grown over this and that for flowering from early July on. Over a delphinium, for instance, whose own flowering ended in early July. We planted five of the mina around a group of 'Mighty Atom', cutting this delphinium back to just below its flowering stems. The short-lived climber soon totally covered the area.

The mina also looks nice with *Verbena bonariensis*, both in flower simultaneously, the verbena light purple, the mina flowers combining yellow, orange and red. The climber's extra weight necessitates staking the verbena.

Alstroemeria ligtu hybrids finish flowering in early July. You pull out all their flowered stems, which frees quite a nice depth of top soil, and one way to treat the vacated space is to grow mina over the peasticks that were lately supporting the ligtus.

ON HEDGES

The star performer here is the flame nasturtium, *Tropaeolum speciosum*, seen at its best in Scotland and the moist West Country. Its tubers run about, so that a colony gradually spreads, and it looks wonderful draping itself over a yew hedge, on which it will flower for many summer weeks. A hedge bottom is generally too dry for it in the south and east, so the cool, moist climate of much of Scotland suits it ideally and it makes garlands of crimson nasturtium flowers. In winter it just melts away, being entirely herbaceous, though supported by its dormant tubers.

ON TREES AND SHRUBS

This is where climbers make their greatest contribution to succession plantings, by clothing trees and shrubs that performed in another season. Here it is most important to match the vigour of the climber with that of its host plant, and to pay attention to what goes on underground. You can't expect a climber (any plant for that matter) to do its job unless it has sufficiently moist and not-too-rooty soil in which to explore. Prepare a really good position with plenty of bulky organic matter in the planting hole. Plant well forward from the host to be climbed over – about 60cm/2ft from the base – and, just as you would against a wall or fence, lead it with string or insulated wire to reach its support. Water well until the climber is established and apply annual surface mulches. Where space is limited, a keen or adventurous gardener (the same

▲ The prolific Clematis
montana *var.* wilsonii
*came to me from my
cousin's garden at Keillour
in Perthshire where it
reached up to the third-
storey roof. At Dixter it is
confined to a single chestnut
pole. It is overwhelmingly
scented of hot chocolate in
its early-summer season.*

▲ ▶ Hydrangea anomala
subsp. petiolaris, *here seen
in Beth Chatto's garden,
has sufficient vigour to
grow up tall trees, provided
there is enough light for its
growth and moisture at the
foot. It flowers in June and
has a second season in the
autumn when its foliage
turns brilliant yellow. If
this can catch autumn sunlight, it is quite transfixing,
but the species does not
demand a sunny aspect.
Give it a start with a not-
too-rooty position and in
well-nourished soil.*

thing, really) will be prepared to start the climber in good compost
in a large wooden container, sited next to the tree trunk and above
ground soil that has at least been scratched around to open it up
a little. Let the container gradually rot.

The host tree must be mature and shrubs need a number of
years to become fully established with a solid framework before
they can cope with the extra burden of a climber. Then you choose
your climber so that it won't overpower its host. You could plant
a rampant *Clematis montana*, for example, near to a tree trunk
to cover the space below the tree's first branches, but the same
clematis would kill a shrub of moderate size. For that you need a
lightweight clematis of no great vigour; one that will perform over
a short period and will then lend itself to being cut away from its
host, so that the latter receives plenty of light once more.

Climbers themselves can play host to others. The versatility of
Hydrangea anomala subsp. *petiolaris* is a notable example. It is self-
clinging, without assistance, and can grow up a wall or tree trunk.
When well established it can then play host to other climbers, say
clematis, growing up it. This last must be capable of being cut
down and removed from the hydrangea at the end of the season.

In a moist climate, *Hydrangea anomala* subsp. *petiolaris* will grow to the top of tall, stemmy trees, as it does up a larch at Inverewe, in northwest Scotland. In the University of Columbia botanic garden, Vancouver, which is right down on the shore-line and has a very wet climate, it grows almost to the top of a Douglas fir tree trunk and has the company with it of *Clematis montana* and of a climbing rose. Quite a combination when you stand back from it, which the situation allows.

A point to notice about this hydrangea is that, over a number of years, its growth will stand further and further forward from its support, whereas you would rather it flowered close to the wall. Very occasionally, I find it advisable, in the winter, to cut the whole lot back to wall level, sacrificing flowers for that season.

Another good succession is formed by growing *Vitis coignetiae* up an ivy, our native *Hedera helix*, itself a self-clinging climber, the host being a wild ash tree, *Fraxinus excelsior*. Because the crown is open and the pinnate foliage light, ash trees make particularly welcoming hosts for climbers such as these. The ivy, having matured, makes non-climbing branches (the leaves now simple, not lobed) that stand out from the tree trunk. In autumn it bears masses of small, green flowers, in umbels. Your attention is drawn to them by the hum of numerous kinds of insects (including wasps), which come for the nectar. Also by the sickly-sweet scent (nothing to moan about). In February its black berries are ripe and they are a great delicacy with wood pigeons. As these are heavy birds, they have difficulty in reaching out for the fruit, and there is a great clatter of wings, as they try to reach their booty while retaining their balance. Quite a laugh, really.

The *Vitis coignetiae* itself has large, rough-textured leaves which should take on glamorous red autumn tints. But both size of leaf and willingness to colour vary greatly in different clones. When purchasing a plant, you need to be fussy. Go in person to the nursery selling them and go in the autumn, when they should be colouring. They will be pot-grown, which in itself often promotes fall colour, but never mind that. If the plant is capable of colouring well at all, it will show it then and you can make your deal. I attach less importance to size of leaf, though it is nice to have large ones.

The vine colours over a very long period – quite six weeks long. It does not colour all at the same time. It is highly visible in early sunshine, as soon as the sun rises, and I admire it from my bathroom about 100m/110yd away. We needn't talk about fruit. That is not the point, though some hardy vines, notably *Vitis* 'Brant', are famed for their fall colour.

▼ *In acquiring* Vitis coignetiae *make sure that you have a form that colours up dramatically in the fall. See it at that time in the nursery where your purchase is made. Here it combines with a mature specimen of our native ivy,* Hedera helix, *which has reached the stage of not climbing any more but flowering abundantly in the autumn when it is covered with wasps and bees. It is a dark but lively green and the two climbers seem perfectly matched – creating a succession of interest in partnership. The vine, colouring in different areas over a period of six weeks, is especially vivid in morning sunlight. I can see it from my bathroom window more than a hundred yards away.*

CLIMBING HONEYSUCKLES

On a very old bay tree, *Laurus nobilis*, already established in the nineteenth century, our wild woodbine, *Lonicera periclymenum*, is an even match, but it is important to go through it annually, in the dormant season (it breaks dormancy very early in the year), to remove old wood, otherwise its bulk and weight become excessive (like mine). This is the best scented (night and early morning) honeysuckle and there are some good named selections, notably 'Serotina' and 'Belgica'.

One of the most popular honeysuckles is *Lonicera japonica* 'Halliana' (if you remember that Hall was a man's name, you won't say it with a short a). The reason often is that it is evergreen – but

pretty horribly shabby in winter, I would comment. This species, which generally starts flowering in late June, carries the season forward into autumn. It will flower on its young, current season's shoots, the flowers borne in axillary pairs, not umbels, like those of our native honeysuckle. They open almost white and deepen to yellow. The night scent is strong, but much more sickly than in *L. periclymenum*.

It is normal practice to hard-prune this honeysuckle in late winter, but if you forbear, it will flower abundantly (and earlier) on its old wood, making a greater show than it ever does on the young. Those who know *L. similis* var. *delavayi*, which is similar in habit, will prefer it. The flowers are a much cleaner white.

All these honeysuckles will flower as happily in shade as in sun. The odourless but showy *L. tragophylla* (yellow) and *L.* × *tellmanniana* (orange) actually prefer shade. I must remember that this is not an essay on climbing honeysuckles but, on the successions theme, should mention *L. caprifolium* (also because I like it), which may be flowering as early as late April. Its flowers are in umbels, pale pink on the outside, creamy within. Another very prolific, umbel-flowered, pink honeysuckle

▲ A rose with the vigour of R. filipes 'Kiftsgate' needs strictly controlling from an early age if it is not to take over completely and occupy an embarrassing amount of space. Here it is growing over a damson plum whose fruit I relish in early September. Perry Rodriguez is seen removing all its flowered wood in March. The long wands of the rose are hooked into the damson as best can be managed without actually tying them. In March–April the tree is full of its own blossom, which is succeeded in July by cascades of scented rose blossom.

that I have enjoyed growing up a pole is *L. × americana*, but with me it seems prone to sudden death. If I replant on the same site, the same fate soon befalls it.

ROSES INTO TREES

The so-called climbing roses are scramblers, making long, wand-like shoots on which they flower in the second year. One of the most famous is *Rosa filipes* 'Kiftsgate', with trusses of white, yellow-stamened flowers in July. They are fragrant on the air. Unpruned, this rose, which is ultra-vigorous, takes up an enormous amount of space, becoming quite an embarrassment. Fore-warned by other people's examples, we prune ours rigorously every year. All its old, flowered shoots are removed and the young ones are guided through the branches of a damson plum, which is the host. This has worked pretty well for a good many years and we get a decent crop of damsons in September. But I would emphasize again that the tree must be mature before it can cope with this extra burden.

Rosa 'Treasure Trove', another rambler and a seedling from 'Kiftsgate' which Graham Thomas (in a good mood) thought worth naming, was raised by John Treasure and has yellower flower trusses. With me, it has a tough assignation. It is planted in dense meadow turf, the idea being to train it into the branches of a huge, white-heart fruiting cherry (food for the birds), so as to bring a little summer interest into the tree in July. We keep a circle cultivated around the rose (which is just beyond the cherry's perimeter) and top-dress with compost in winter. But the spot becomes desperately dry in summer and is never watered, not being handy for a supply. The rose receives an annual pruning and its young shoots are encouraged by being tied to connecting string, to reach into the cherry branches. It has taken years to achieve this but, hurrah!, it has got there at last. Will the entire cherry crown be garlanded in roses some day? What a dream – but it is hope that keeps us going.

VERSATILE CLEMATIS

As well as the clematis already mentioned, we have many others growing over shrubs and as vertical features on poles. In the Long Border *C*. 'Jackmanii Superba' goes up into, or rather over, the bulky framework of the August–September-flowering privet, *Ligustrum quihoui*. The purple clematis flowers first, from late June, and there is a little overlap with the privet. So long as we can (with

A succession that we are proud of is the winter-flowering Mahonia × media *'Buckland' with the* Clematis flammula *hybrid, C. × triternata 'Rubromarginata'.*

▲ *The first necessity is to ensure that the mahonia is a really solid bush before it has the weight of the clematis on it, which means pruning in the spring, before growth is renewed, to develop a framework that becomes increasingly chunky. Plant the clematis a good 30cm/1ft away from the mahonia's overhang and keep it fed and watered until established.*

chemicals) keep the clematis from going down to powdery mildew halfway through its flowering season, this works a treat. As we want it to climb quite high into the privet, we do not cut the clematis as hard back, when it comes to pruning, as we might, but start it at 1.5m/5ft or so. This type of clematis flowers on its current season's growth. When this dies off, in November, it clings to its now dead and brown leaves and looks hideous, which is insupportable, so we cut it back there and then. No harm done, I promise. We prune the privet in the dead of winter, 29 January this year (it is 30 January as I write). A good winter job.

We enjoy bunches of yellow flowers in midwinter on *Mahonia × media* 'Buckland'. What about the rest of the year? It is easy to drape a clematis over its whorls of evergreen foliage, but the mahonia cannot flourish in darkness, or even in deep gloom, for

▲ *The* Clematis × t. *'Rubromarginata' is not excessively heavy or overwhelming; it is its fragrance that overwhelms. As soon as it has flowered in July, it can be cut off its host to bide its time till the following spring.*

very long. The clematis we have chosen to do the job has proved ideal. It is *C.* × *triternata* 'Rubromarginata', with small, cruciform, whitish flowers margined in reddish mauve. It has a tremendous fragrance (derived from *C. flammula*) on the air. Flowering in August, on its young growth, it mantles the mahonia quite lightly (that is the point) and, as soon as the show is over, we cut it back. 'With one bound, Tarzan was free.' Whenever this mahonia (and others like it) makes rather long, stemmy shoots, we cut them back in early spring, which makes for a sturdy, solid bush that will take the weight of a climber over it. But the mahonia was mature before we monkeyed about with it.

We have some old espalier 'Doyenné du Comice' (the judging committee's top choice) pears throughout our High Garden, a relic of my father's great love for pears. Apart from annual spur

pruning, they get no attention (we replace them from time to time) and are covered with lichens. They make a perfect framework for climbers to enliven. We planted a 'Bill MacKenzie' clematis (a vigorous, yellow-flowered hybrid, related to *C. tangutica*) over one pear. The pear was killed. Here endeth the first lesson. But the South African *C. brachiata* placed in the same situation worked well. It starts late into growth and is never heavy. Similarly, the ruse works with a range of large-flowered clematis hybrids, especially those that flower on their old wood, in May–June. Better than I deserve, I get some delicious pears, though they are scabby in a wet season.

Thladiantha dubia, from China, is an original and it is a thug. You have to work to stop it taking over, but it does look super, in September, mantling a couple of aged but lusty *Cistus × cyprius* that have passed their summer prime. Thladiantha seems to be just about the only member of the cucumber family (*Cucurbitaceae*) that we can grow as a hardy perennial outdoors. It overwinters with fleshy tubers and these increase their range at panic-striking speed (don't worry; you'll cope, but I have to warn you). Like that of other cucurbits, its summer growth has climbing tendrils and it travels far and wide. Three times in a season we have to pull it off the cistuses, to stop them being choked. But in September it is a mass of tiny, yellow cucumber flowers. No one has a clue what it is, but everyone is fascinated. The clone in cultivation is male, so there are no fruits, which is probably just as well, but I should rather like to see a pollinated female, hung with fruit.

ANNUAL AND TENDER CLIMBERS

These are useful for all sorts of succession purposes – among them the already cited *Mina lobata* (syn. *Ipomoea lobata*), brought on in pots or plugs, tucked round perennials that have done their stuff by mid July. This is a stalwart with us, whereas success or otherwise with *Ipomoea tricolor* 'Heavenly Blue' is always something of a toss-up. It hates the cold and goes pinched and yellow if submitted to it in May. So we sow pretty late but the display goes on pretty late in a good season. Rain rather ruins a newly opened flush of blossom. All being well, a new crop of these opens every morning and the open-mouthed trumpets are thrillingly sky blue. You must go out and admire them before the show is over at midday, when they first turn mauvish and then crumple. Fergus dots the plants all over the place and they completely and delightfully take me by surprise when I first notice them. One of the greatest successes was over the top of the privet, *Ligustrum* 'Vicaryi', at the

◀ Thladiantha dubia *is a hardy member of the cucumber family which overwinters with tubers and is quite an aggressive spreader. All is forgiven in September when it is a mass of yellow blossom, male blossom, I should say, since the female does not seem to be in cultivation, but if it were it would weigh everything to the ground. The old clematis 'Ville de Lyon' has joined in the party. Whatever they are growing over is having a tough time of it.*

▼ Ligustrum 'Vicaryi' *has a long season, its lime, evergreen foliage being the main point, but it flowers well in June (the flowered wood should then be removed). As a bon bouche we have mantled it on this occasion with the annual morning glory, Ipomoea tricolor 'Heavenly Blue', which gives you a delightful bolt from the blue every morning in summer and early autumn.*

back of the Long Border. The foliage on this privet is yellow-green and perfect behind the blue climber.

Bomarea caldasii belongs to *Alstroemeriaceae* and looks like an alstroemeria. It is a twining climber and its flowers are borne in generous clusters on the ends of current season's shoots. That is rather too late in the season, but in Helen Dillon's Dublin garden, one June, I enviously admired a specimen that had brought its old growth through the winter and carried masses of bloom. The trumpet-shaped flowers are deep, rich orange. Mine is guided up sticks till it reaches into the stiff, horizontal branches of a *Cotoneaster horizontalis* that has seeded itself into the top of an old wall and brackets out from it. The bomarea thrives on warmth and shelter. It may behave like a herbaceous perennial, if cut back by cold weather in the winter, but generally returns. Sometimes it ripens seed, which germinates readily.

Rhodochiton atrosanguineus is an unlikely member of *Scrophulariaceae* – a twining climber that is best treated as a tender biennial, to give it a good start and to help it towards early flowering in the following year. Rarely, old plants survive the winter outside. It drapes itself where it will and is effective in front of the blue, juvenile foliage of a seedling *Eucalyptus gunnii*. We also have a photographic record of its purple trail hanging across a leaf of the yellow-and-green-striped *Canna* 'Striata'. The lantern-like flowers are in two visible parts. The outer calyx is the lantern, and pale purple. It persists for weeks. The much more ephemeral corolla is tubular and very dark purple. White stamens peep coyly from its mouth. This part drops away in quite a short while. It is a fascinating plant, not hearty and coarsely robust but light, with thread-like stems.

Now *Cobaea scandens* is a coarse and hearty climber. The problem in growing it is to get it sufficiently advanced early on to flower freely before autumn puts a stop to it. But if a wall has suddenly and unexpectedly developed a gap (the ceanothus died), cobaea will do a rapid filling-in job. It carries well-displayed bells of purple flowers (slightly dirty purple) or there is a green-flowered variant, *Cobaea scandens* f. *alba*, sought after by gardeners with good taste. Best germination is from seeds from your own plant. These seldom ripen in time, so you should collect a pod with some stalk behind it and stand it in water indoors, in a light place where it will probably ripen in January. Remember, though, that cobaea sometimes survives the winter. Or you can root cuttings taken in early autumn.

I have written about *Lathyrus grandiflorus*, but not of the everlasting pea, *L. latifolius* (which people will persistently call everlasting sweet pea, though it is entirely without scent), which is a general favourite, though rather a nasty shade of pink in the type-plant. However, the pure white 'Albus' is a lovely thing, as is the larger-flowered 'White Pearl'. I have the latter growing through a vigorous, pink Hybrid Tea rose and it is always a pleasure to welcome it back. It is a persistent herbaceous perennial with nothing tricksy about it. Grow it and if it turns out to be pink after all, as seedlings can do, throw it out forthwith.

The main contribution made by climbers is to prolong a plant's season of interest and to intensify the many-faceted picture you are creating.

Bomarea caldasii
Height: 3–4m/10–12ft
Sun or part-shade, moist
but well-drained soil
Needs protection
This twining climber has
attractive, narrow leaves.
The trumpet-shaped
flowers are deep, rich
orange, speckled inside,
and borne in clusters on
the ends of the current
season's shoots, in July
with me. Guide up sticks
till it reaches into its host.
Normally, the first autumn
frost cuts bomarea down
to the ground, but it re-
appears in late spring.

◄ **Clematis 'Bill
MacKenzie'**
Height: 5m/16ft
Hardy, sun or shade
A vigorous clematis that
will swamp anything less
than an extremely strong
host or a supporting post
firmly anchored. You'll
need to tie in the stems to
keep it in line. The lemon-
yellow, lantern-like flowers
are produced *en masse*
from June to October,
being joined mid-season
by the silky seed heads
of the flowers that came
first. Prune hard or lightly
to suit the situation and
the space. It can travel
a long distance. Light
pruning will enable
flowering to start in June
with no loss of flower
power at the tail end.

▼ **Clematis 'Madame
Julia Correvon'**
Height: 4m/12ft
Spread: 1m/3ft
Hardy, sun or shade
The late-flowering viticella
clematis flower from June
to September. We grow
'Madame Julia Correvon',
which is wine red with
creamy yellow anthers,
up a chestnut pole. Other
viticella hybrids include:
'Etoile Violette', purple
with a prominent white
centre, and one of the
earliest to flower; and
'Purpurea Plena Elegans',
with double flowers the
colour of old roses. If it
is grown up a living host,
remove some of the
clematis growth in
December to give the tree
or shrub enough light to
recover during the winter
months, then give the
final hard prune during
February.

Clematis montana
Height and spread: up to
9m/30ft
Hardy, top in sun, roots
in shade
Clematis montana and
its hybrids, the Montana
Group, are too
rampageous to drape
over a living support
other than a large tree,
but are useful on poles
and high walls. They
flower in early summer
and, once established,
need only a tidy up rather
than a prune. I'm fond of
C. 'Freda', a good pink
form with pale anthers
and dark green or
bronzed leaves. She
doesn't take off at the
same rate as *C. montana*
var. *wilsonii*, which
creates cascades of
powerfully sweet-scented,
white blossom.

Clematis recta 'Purpurea'
Height: 1–2.25m/3–7ft
Hardy, sun
A truly herbaceous clem-
atis; the young shoots
in spring are purple yet
silvery on the undersides.
We delay giving them
support for as long as
we dare, but then make
a substantial framework
of brushwood, to 2.25m/
7ft, to truss up the clematis' vigorous but feeble
stems. Its pinnate leaves
clasp weakly and are
dark green by the time
of flowering. The tiny
flowers are white and
foam abundantly, but
not for long. Immediately
after the display, shear
the plant over, and you
may get a secondary
crop of young leaves
and flowers. Alternatively,
leave it for its seed heads.

▲ **Cobaea scandens
f. alba**
Cathedral bells
Height and spread:
10–20m/33–70ft
Tender, sun or part-shade
The ideal vigorous
climber to plug a gap or

to scramble over ever-
greens, as long as you've
sown seed early enough
for the green-white or
purple bells to flower
before the plant is cut
short by the first frost. In
well-protected gardens,

cobaea may come
through the winter. If you
prefer to propagate by
root cuttings, remember
to take them in early
autumn. Early sowing
promotes earlier than the
normal late flowering.

perfectly well.) In winter its bare young stems are coloured warm cinnamon, while next year's leaf buds are already green. A nice contrast.

◀ *Ipomoea* (syn. *Mina*) *lobata*
Spanish flag
Height: 2–5m/6–16ft
Tender, sun
This tender climber (from Mexico) can be sown in late winter under protection or in spring for a late contribution. We use it to mask the remains of perennials, such as delphiniums, and to enhance *Verbena bonariensis*, setting stakes around the principals so as to prevent the whole edifice from collapsing. The mina has clusters of tubular, crimson, orange-and-yellow flowers on crimson stems.

▲ *Ipomoea tricolor* **'Heavenly Blue'**
Morning glory
Height: 2m/6ft
Tender, sun
The large trumpet flowers make a dazzling show. According to when it is sown – early or late – it will flower between June and September. Grow over any support where they are not crowded out.

We pop them in all over the place to give us surprises. You'll never, in our climate, see too many of them as they are quite tricky to grow well. We sow in early May under glass and get them outdoors in late June.

Hydrangea anomala subsp. *petiolaris*
Climbing hydrangea
Height and spread: indefinite
Hardy, moist leaf soil in sun or shade
Deciduous, self-clinging and vigorous enough once established to play host to other climbers, such as clematis that are cut back annually. White, lacecap flowers come (rather briefly, I have to admit) in June. In autumn its foliage changes to a wonderful clear yellow, especially if given a sunny position. (This species is often recommended for north walls, on which it performs

▼ *Lathyrus latifolius* **'White Pearl'**
Everlasting pea
Height: 2m/6ft or more
Hardy, sun
The pure white perennial pea is in a different league from the pink type-plant. Grow it through a vigorous rose, such as 'Meizeli' (The McCartney Rose). Its racemes of white pea flowers join the rose's pink blossom from midsummer onwards.

▶ *Lonicera periclymenum* **'Serotina'**
Late Dutch honeysuckle
Height: 7m/22ft
Hardy, sun
I have this vigorous honeysuckle as a pole feature and prune it annually by removing all its flowered (and fruited) growth. The long, unbranched new shoots are left intact, merely tied into the pole here and there. Its main season is June–July but there are flowering aftermaths through to autumn. The colour varies – at its best the outside of the flower is deep red, while the inside is cream. Early Dutch honeysuckle, *L. p.* 'Belgica', has white flowers that turn cream with red streaks. They are all selections from the wildings in Dutch Guelderland, so they are apt to vary widely.

Rhodochiton atrosanguineus
Height: 3m/10ft
Tender, sun
With pendent, lantern-like, purple flowers on thread-like stems, this twining climber is a useful adjunct to roses, perennials and other climbers. It drapes where it will without harming its host. Sow in the autumn, bring on under glass and plant out in spring.

Tropaeolum speciosum
Flame nasturtium
Height: 3–5m/10–16ft
Hardy, partial shade, cool acid soil
The climbing nasturtium from Chile has decorative, six-lobed leaves. The brilliant red flowers are born continuously in late summer. It is especially effective against a dark host. In winter it melts away, being entirely herbaceous.

A matter of
MAINTENANCE

A plant's good health is the start to good gardening. If it is happy, it will give of its best, encouraging a longer season of display.

Start by making sure the ground is 'in good heart', to use an old phrase. It must be well drained but also have water-holding capacity. The way to ensure that is to incorporate plenty of well-rotted, bulky organic matter, like garden compost. And you need to add this, throughout the border's life, in generous quantities. The best, farmyard manure that is so well rotted as to have ceased to smell, is not easily obtained. But you keep it as an ideal at the back of your mind.

It is a help to know the history and provenance of the compost and manure you use. If it has been in a heap outside surrounded by stinging nettles or other tiresome weeds, they will have seeded into it and will give you trouble for years afterwards. This applies also to mushroom compost, the compost in which a crop of mushrooms was grown but which can be used only once and is thereafter turned out into a heap – vulnerable again to what has been allowed to seed into it before it reaches you.

A lot of lime has to be added to mushroom compost, to prevent its being too acid, and this will still be largely present in the sample that you use for your plants. Some of these will be lime haters, that is calcifuge (fleeing from calcium). If you apply mushroom compost to such plants, they will turn yellow and become sickly. We need to learn which plants are susceptible and to apply some other bulky organic dressing to them, like well-rotted, finely ground-up

◀ *Clods in the snow. Before planting we need to get our heavy clay soil into a condition that makes it manageable (for us gardeners) and good for plants since it allows their roots greater access to nutrients. Areas we plan to plant or replant in the spring are single dug (to one spit, the depth of a spade) in the autumn and left over winter. Exposure to frosts and snow helps break down large clods. This, hand in hand with the addition of organic matter and crushed horticultural grit, improves the soil structure and keeps it healthy.*

▲ Most spades have a blade 25cm/10in long, the depth needed when digging one spit deep. A good, sharp spade that is easy to handle and comfortable to use makes digging a more pleasurable experience. True, it is hard work creating a well-prepared bed, but also satisfying. Digging in the rain is grim, however, both for the digger and the dug, since working on saturated ground can cause it to lose its structure.

We lift and turn clods over (centre) and either leave them to be broken down by winter frosts or break them down with a garden fork as we go. Churning up the soil is more easily achieved with a rotavator, but use of this machine on the same ground can cause an impenetrable pan, which has to be broken down by hand digging.

Having worked in organic matter and grit, we use the garden fork (right) to work the soil into a fine tilth ready for planting. A crumbly, even-textured soil is what we aim for.

bark. This will be more expensive than mushroom compost. There's always a snag lurking around the corner. Still, you are very abstemious in other aspects of the way you live; you don't smoke; perhaps you don't drink, at least not spirits. There must be some plus values to your way of life which will enable you to rationalize any hesitation you might have entertained regarding the expense of looking after your plants in the best way possible.

Many gardeners, albeit tender-hearted, do not recognize the symptoms when their plants are starved. If they don't grow well, these people will simply plant more of them and closer together. Whereas a few really healthy plants would meet the situation and do them credit.

You don't want to lean heavily on artificial fertilizers, because they add no value to the structure of the soil and their stimulus is ephemeral. But they do sometimes come in handy as a short-term boost to growth at a time when the plant can make use of it – generally in spring. And there are good slow-release fertilizers, which operate over a considerable period. This period can nowadays be gauged quite accurately. If, for instance, you want it to last for six months, taking the plant from spring to autumn, when it is in greatest need of sustenance, there will be a fertilizer to meet this requirement. A word of warning: frost destroys the slow-release mechanism of these fertilizers, so that they release it all suddenly and at one go, with disastrous results.

The depth of your top soil, which is the most nutritious, should

▲ A handful of material off the compost heap that has not rotted down effectively. To make good compost, you need a balance of strawy material to green, with plenty of water, air and lime to counteract the acidity caused by decomposition. Regular turning of the heap allows air to get in and speeds up the whole process.

Well-rotted compost is dark, crumbly and sweet-smelling (centre). Our home-made stuff is by no means sterile or free of weed seeds, so we take care

where we use it and generally confine it to the vegetable garden. For the borders, I prefer a sterile medium. Mushroom compost increases the alkalinity of the soil, so needs careful handling. Around acid-loving plants we use a ground microchip, which is part composted and fine-textured.

We never put down a mulch in the borders because it prevents self-sowers from germinating. Instead we tickle in compost around the plants (right), bringing some soil to the surface in the process.

be taken into account. Perhaps the subsoil, 15cm/6in down, is nasty, sticky clay, into which plant roots will not be encouraged to explore. The more extensive a plant's root system, the stronger and healthier it will be. There are various ways of dealing with this situation and you should get expert advice on which will be best for you.

I have already commented on the attractions and disadvantages of bark mulches.

REGULAR UPKEEP

If the ground is well prepared and unless you have allowed weeds to get out of control, it will never be necessary to take everything out of a mixed border and start again. All ground work – weeding, planting, splitting, dividing, replanting and so on – will be on a piecemeal basis. Deal with a small stretch at a time, finishing the job before the night's rain or frost sets in. If the job is left half done, the soil condition may be ruined for planting because the ground is like a sponge and rain will stop play the next day.

The stronger the plant, the more resilience it will have to serve you well and over a long period. A let-alone policy will seldom achieve this. If a plant or colony of plants is just left undisturbed over a considerable time, it will deteriorate through congestion and provide you with a far shorter season of being at its best than is necessary.

When it comes to shrubs, you can again ensure that they are kept young and healthy. You must cut out old, tired or dead wood

1   2   3

▲ *A liberal use of water is the basis of successful planting, especially of container-grown plants from nurseries and garden centres, as peat- or peat-substitute-based composts dry out rapidly.* **1** *Soak the plant thoroughly by plunging it in a bucket of water until bubbles cease to appear on the surface. Meanwhile dig a hole at least twice the width of the plant's rootball.* **2** *Remove the plant from the bucket and take it out of its container.*

3 Gently tease apart roots that have become coiled or compressed as this will encourage them to be adventurous. **4** *Stand the plant in the hole and fill in around it with soil. Water thoroughly.* **5** *Gently firm in the soil with your hands (not your heel) to get rid of unwanted air pockets, making sure that the plant is neither too deeply planted nor too shallow (follow the nursery mark indicating soil level). Water thoroughly again.*

so that the plant can rejuvenate itself. You have let light into the centre of the bush and that will enable it to make fresh young growth from low down, but this must go hand in hand with generous feeding and watering. You have also reduced the size of the bush, which owed its bulk to a lot of inert growth at its centre. That will leave more space for further planting.

Do you realize how generous watering needs to be in order to be effective? It does not mean just sprinkling from a hose as you pass. To be thorough and to reach down to the shrub's lowest roots, a watering may need to be continuous for a couple of hours. Naturally, to leave the water on overnight is a wicked waste. Good gardening needs thought and concentration, not just lurching from one extreme to the opposite.

▶ *Efficient hand-weeding requires that you should get down to it with a sharp-pointed, sharp-edged, stainless-steel trowel (right). And I mean get down – on your knees, with a soft rubber mat for comfort. This way your eyes are close to the ground and you can be sure – well, more sure – of what to remove and what to leave. My policy is to leave a seedling until I can identify it. And with self-sowers, you want to edit rather than delete wholesale, which makes precision weeding essential.*

A Dutch hoe (far right) is the answer for gardeners who like to weed from a standing position, but is hard to use with precision when weeding among garden plants. The long-handled hoe is useful for chopping the tops off crops of annual weeds, such as chickweed and groundsel. Hoeing needs to be done when the weather is dry, otherwise weeds will reroot and you'll be wasting your time.

4

5

▼ There are no hard-and-fast rules for pruning, every case being different, except for these: always use the appropriate tool for the task and make sure it is sharp, so that it cuts easily, cleanly and safely. A blunt cutting instrument can leave ragged wounds that are prone to infection.

Secateurs (below left) are useful for pruning woody stems. Cut to just above a bud so as not to leave any nasty snags. Loppers (below centre) with long handles enable you to cut thicker stems and branches that may be difficult to reach with secateurs. A pruning saw (below right) with hardpoint, heat-treated teeth can be used on branches too thick to cut with loppers.

DEAD-HEADING

There is an on-going need for dead-heading, to keep a border looking fresh right to the end of the season – the last day of October, let us say, for northern-hemisphere gardeners. In some cases, but only some, removal of flower heads that are running to seed will relieve the plant of expending useless energy, thereby stimulating it into making more flower buds.

A trial of *Helenium* at Wisley confirmed what we already suspected, that the old variety 'Moerheim Beauty' has more staying power than almost any of the modern cultivars. Although its flower shape is nothing to boast about, it is a good bronze. Its first wave of blossom comes in late June and July. After that it pauses for breath, but it will soon be seen that a new crop of flower buds

is developing further down the stems. We have only to remove the faded heads, taking them back to where new, developing buds can be seen. If none is visible, as is likely at the centre of a flowering complex, the stem is removed to a lower level. But the second crop of blossom, in late August and September, will be almost as showy as the first. *Anthemis tinctoria*, available in a range of cultivars, is another example, but of a slightly different kind. I discussed it in the first chapter.

On the trial ground at Wisley we have found that many perennials benefit from being replanted every year, using single young shoots as softwood cuttings, to get them started. Monardas have been martyrs to mildew, of recent years; by this treatment they will escape. So will Michaelmas daisies of the *Aster novae-belgii* type.

Keeping your plants young will also have the advantage of preventing them turning brown and looking senile prematurely. There was an example of this in the double herbaceous borders made by Piet Oudolf at Wisley. By August they were already going off and by September were really tired and brown. We want our borders to look fresh and lively to the end of October. Winter is

▼ *Dead-heading is necessary for immediate appearance. It may also perform the additional function of forcing the plant to flower again. Helenium 'Moerheim Beauty' has a first flush at the end of June (below left), but this variety is capable of further effort.*

If the first flush is removed as it fades, a second flush lower down the plant will be stimulated into action, flowering in August (far below right). A photograph of the helenium taken on the same date, but where plants were not dead-headed, shows the effect of not bothering (below right).

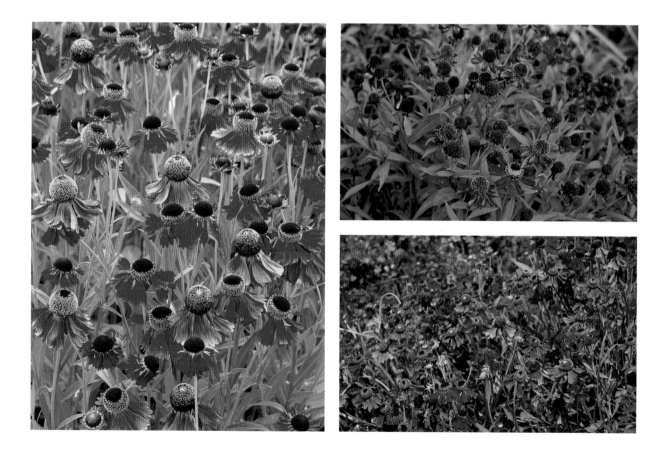

▲ *The border is still looking fresh and colourful in August, but too many brown plants could drag it into autumn prematurely. Here, just one teazel, Dipsacus sylvestris, is weighty enough to give us the necessary effect, both now and as a skeleton through the winter. The* rest have been removed. In the first year, these biennial teazels make a ground-hugging rosette of green leaves. Thin these out rigorously, keeping the strongest, which will be the ones that recieve the most light – generally those at the border's margin.

early enough to be welcoming brown as a colour. Earlier than that, continual dead-heading is necessary. And it becomes a pleasure, when you enjoy the results and (rather meanly) compare your garden with the gardens of people who gave up early.

Teazels are all very well while fresh – good structure, interesting flowers. But as soon as they have finished flowering in mid-August, they start turning brown. Get rid of ninety per cent of them immediately and leave only ten per cent for winter skeletons.

STAKING

If you don't stake, and stake in time, plants will collapse and never look the same again, even if you prop them up after it has happened. Within hours of falling, their tops will have turned upwards at a right-angle and this can never be corrected. If you leave them lying on the ground, the squashed look will be terrible, not to mention interfering with their neighbours. You will feel inclined to cut them down or pull them out immediately. End of summer in the border, possibly a couple of months before it need be.

Far more staking is practised in a mixed border than you would ever suspect – if it is well done and invisible. The staking agents are peasticks, alias brushwood, or bamboo canes.

Peasticks need to be sharpened to a point at the base and you must have enough unbranched stick at the base to plunge it deeply and firmly into the soil. This, in its turn, needs to be soft and moist enough to enable deep plunging. Peasticks are not decorative objects in themselves and should not, if possible, be inserted too long before the plants will need them. So at Dixter we do our sticking on a piecemeal basis and over a period. In the double borders at Wisley all the peasticks are put in in one fell swoop, which means that they will be disagreeably visible for longer before plant growth conceals them all. But Wisley is an institution, and to get the students doing the entire job at a go is practical. Afterwards they can all be moved on to some other job. Fine tuning is practical only in a private garden. You always want to look behind you after doing any job and criticize the way you have left it.

Use plenty of peasticks; don't be stingy with them so that parts of the plant escape and fall outwards. If the ground was hard so that you couldn't get the sticks in deep enough, it may be a good idea to run a bit of string around the entire cage of sticks at the end, securing it here and there, but the sticks should always remain vertical and not be pulled inwards. Plant shoots themselves always grow vertically. You must anticipate how high each plant group will

eventually grow and make sure that your sticks will be long and
strong enough to support it when fully grown and top-heavy with
flowers or rainwater. The novice will nearly always underestimate.

Now for the canes, which are the alternative method of support
(unless you use horizontally supported wide-mesh netting, which
I should abominate myself, for reasons that I hope I have already
made obvious: in three words, lack of flexibility). Canes are made
of bamboo and can be purchased in a range of lengths and thick-
nesses. The thicker they are, the more obtrusive they will be, but
they must be man enough for the job without bending under the
weight imposed on them.

They must also be strong enough not to snap, to which they
become more prone with repeated use. If re-using old canes, test
their strength before you start by applying weight to them. If they
snap, you will still be able to trim them back at the base and use
them again for lower jobs. When new, bamboo canes are shiny and
bright yellow, which can be far too distracting in a border context.
Try to use them, in the first year, where their colour won't matter
– for instance, supporting outdoor tomatoes.

Two points that may seem obvious to you and to me but that
often set my teeth on edge in a novice's hands: the canes must be
inserted right way up. They came from living plants and all canes
are thicker at the lower end than at the top. Second, they *must go
in vertically* because they look dreadful if leaning this way and that.

Use enough canes. Don't put an excess burden on them by
using too few. With a single stem, or even two, to support, as it
might be delphinium, one cane put in behind, where it won't be
seen, may be sufficient. More stems, more canes (but don't overdo
them!). Get them in firmly. In hard ground we make a prelimin-
ary hole by knocking in a length of angle-iron and then removing it.

TIES

What you use for making your ties will largely depend on how heavy a job is in question. For something really heavy, like cardoon flowering stems, you will need strong posts and maybe as strong tying material as insulated wire. For lighter work, there are plenty of tying strings to choose from on the market. Not an obtrusive colour, please.

Suppose it is a ball or reel of some sort of string. My own method is to unwind a manageable length of this and, leaving a length free, to secure it to the support with a clove hitch. This will never slip. Now, with the free end, I take the string around the outside of the plant stems, securing it to a stem from time to time by twisting round it, then on to the next cane, making another twist (or clove hitch) around that until, if I have judged the length of string needed correctly, I come back to where I started and finish off with a reef knot. One circuit may be enough for the season, but a second, at a higher level, may be needed when the plant has grown taller. I leave my plants unstaked for as long as I dare, without them blowing over, so as to minimize the number of times they will need retying. There are various ways of doing the job. Choose your own, as long as it is effective and invisible.

If the plant group is large, there will be a number of canes and, having made your outer circuit, you will need to take your string across from one cane to another that crosses the diameter of the circle. An extra cane or two may be needed within the circle. Criss-crossing several times, you will end up with a cat's cradle within your original circuit. The plant stems will not be held rigid but will be able to move and give way to the wind, but to a limited degree. Stems should never be tied in tightly to their support, else they will have no free play and will be liable to snap off.

I briefly referred, in the first chapter, to the way Fergus copes with *Miscanthus sinensis* 'Silberfeder' (Silver Feather) when it is blown, by prevailing southerly winds, away from your viewpoint. The border faces south and your viewpoint is from the south. You want the grass to face you. He stakes it in the usual way except at the front, where stakes would show. There he drives the canes in at 45 degrees, so that they enter the ground behind the colony (on its north side). All that is visible from your viewpoint at the front is the very tip of the canes. This is where the string is attached, though it continues its circuit attached to vertical canes not visible from the front anyway.

▼ *Secure your twine to the cane with a clove hitch, leaving a free end of generous length – enough to encircle the entire plant without drawing the stems together. Pass this around each stem as you come to it and twist it back on itself before proceeding to the* next stem. *Complete the circuit with a reef knot made to the ball end of the string. Here Fergus is using 3-ply tarred fillis to tie a single rose stem to a cane. We use 3- or 5-ply fillis, tarred or untarred, according to the strength needed for the job.*

INDEX

Page numbers in *italic* refer to the illustrations and captions.

Good teamwork: Ipomoea
(*syn.* Mina) lobata *in*
flower simultaneously with
Verbena bonariensis,
the verbena light purple,
the mina flowers combining
yellow, orange and red.
The climber's extra weight
necessitates staking the
verbena.

ACKNOWLEDGEMENTS

Jonathan Buckley with his photographs and Erica Hunningher with her editing have made a big contribution. I must also thank Perry Rodriguez, my business manager, Ken Wilson, the designer, Tony Lord for checking nomenclature, and Viv Bowler, my commissioning editor at the BBC, who has been supportive and encouraging throughout.

If the book is a success, which of course it has to be, it is Fergus Garrett who deserves more than anyone a big share in its reflected glory. He is the unsung hero and has given me an enormous slice of his time and creative thought with no recompense other than my unstinted gratitude. Thank you, Fergus.